YORK NO

York Notes Rapid Revision

AQA English Language Paper 2

Written by Emma Scott-Stevens

Pearson

YORK PRESS

YORK PRESS
322 Old Brompton Road, London SW5 9JH

PEARSON EDUCATION LIMITED
80 Strand, London, WC2R 0RL

10 9 8 7 6 5 4 3 2 1

ISBN 978–1–2922–7095–1

Phototypeset by Kamae Design
Printed in Slovakia

Text credits:
'The Ocean is Broken' by Greg Ray, reproduced by permission of the author. 'Why
our care homes open their doors at Christmas to lonely older people' © Guardian
News & Media Ltd 2019.

Photo credits:
Lapina/Shutterstock for page 7 bottom / North Wind Picture Archives/Alamy for
page 9 bottom / andras_csontos/Shutterstock for page 10 bottom / nano/© iStock
for page 13 bottom / BrianAJackson/© iStock for page 14 bottom / Pressmaster/
Shutterstock for page 18 top / CherylRamalho/Shutterstock for page 21 bottom /
Rich Carey/Shutterstock for page 25 bottom / Atomic/Alamy for page 26 bottom /
VH-studio/Shutterstock for page 30 bottom / JasonOndreicka/© iStock for page 32
bottom / gemenacom/© iStock for page 34 centre / Alvey & Towers Picture Library/
Alamy for page 35 centre / Sergey Kamshylin/Shutterstock for page 37 bottom
/ Africa Studio/Shutterstock for page 38 centre / tongo51/Shutterstock for page
39 centre and 39 bottom / mentatdgt/Shutterstock for page 40 bottom / Maslov
Dmitry/Shutterstock for page 42 bottom / Design Pics Inc/Alamy for page 45 bottom
/ Bohbeh/Shutterstock for page 46 bottom / michaeljung/Shutterstock for page
49 bottom / travelview/Shutterstock for page 51 centre / Ben Parker/Shutterstock
for page 52 bottom / Iakov Filimonov/Shutterstock for page 55 bottom / Ms Jane
Campbell/Shutterstock for page 57 centre / Steve Debenport/© iStock for page 63
bottom / didesign021/Shutterstock for page 71 bottom / 19th era 2/Alamy for
page 73 top

CONTENTS

INTRODUCTION What's it all about?

What do I need to know to begin?

This Rapid Revision book takes you through all the skills you need to know for both parts of the exam paper. These skills are ALL linked to the Assessment Objectives. Assessment Objectives (or AOs) are the skills you need to demonstrate to the marker or examiner in order to succeed.

Three key things about Assessment Objectives

1. You will be assessed through **six** AOs – **AO1, AO2, AO3** and **AO4** relate to the **Reading section** of the exam; **AO5** and **AO6** to the **Writing section**.

2. **Specific questions** target **particular AOs** – make sure you know what is being targeted. We have provided AO references in each unit to help you.

3. Some AOs are **worth more in marks than others**, but none are worth ignoring!

What are the AOs for Section A: Reading?

Read through the information in the table below to become more familiar with the area covered by each Assessment Objective.

AO1	AO2	AO3	AO4
• Identify and interpret explicit and implicit information and ideas • Select and synthesise evidence from different texts	Explain, comment on and analyse how writers use language and structure to achieve effects and influence readers, using relevant subject terminology to support their views	Compare writers' ideas and perspectives, as well as how these are conveyed, across two or more texts	Evaluate texts critically and support this with appropriate textual references

What are the AOs for Section B: Writing?

AO5	AO6
• Communicate clearly, effectively and imaginatively, selecting and adapting tone, style and register for different forms, purposes and audiences • Organise information and ideas, using structural and grammatical features to support coherence and cohesion of texts	Use a range of vocabulary and sentence structures for clarity, purpose and effect, with accurate spelling and punctuation. (20% of total marks)

How will my Rapid Revision book help me master these AOs?

Units **will explain clearly** what the core skill is

⬇

'Putting it into practice' **shows how** how to 'hit' the AO

⬇

'How can you approach it?' **breaks the skill down into** steps

⬇

'Now you try it' gives you the chance to **apply what you have learned**

Tasks labelled **Q** develop your exam skills; tasks with numbers offer practice questions. The **Quick revision** section at the **end of each chapter** (pages 20, 44 and 58) will make sure you have really mastered the AOs. Longer **sample student responses** at Grades 5 and 7+ in the Exam Practice section will also give you an idea of how the AOs can be targeted effectively.

The **full exam practice tasks** (pages 22–29 and 60–69) and **Practice paper 2** (pages 70–74) will give you the chance to tackle the AOs as part of a whole assessment.

Good luck – and **enjoy** your revision!

What will you be asked?

- **Question 1** is worth **4 marks**.
- It will ask you to **read** a **clearly identified section** from **one source**.
- You will be given **eight statements** about this section of the text. You need to decide **which four statements about the section are true**.
- You will need to **shade in the boxes** for the four correct statements.

What should you look for?

- First **find the section** that is **identified in the question** and draw a box around it to make sure you **focus on this section only**.
- Then **read the section closely** and **read the statements** in the answer booklet.
- Search for **key words or ideas** in the statement that you can see in the text.

Putting it into practice

Read this extract from Source A. It is about a family eating their dinner.

> *After we quickly devoured our plates of food, there was yet more waiting. Then we sat quietly at the table, whilst orders were taken for dessert. However, dessert was eaten very slowly as we all realised that washing up came next.*

Q: Now read the statement below. Is it true?

A The writer always ate all of her food really quickly, especially dessert.

How can you approach it?

- Identify the key words and ideas in the statement (highlighted below).

  A The writer always ate all of her food really quickly, especially dessert.

- Find the sections of the text that relate to the key words and ideas (highlighted below).

  'After we quickly devoured our piled high plates of food… However, dessert was eaten very slowly…'

- Ask yourself: Is this statement correct? No, it is not correct because the writer did not eat *all* her food quickly. Her dessert was eaten 'very slowly'.
- Move on to the next statement and follow the process again.

Now you try!

Read the first part of Source A below from lines 1 to 10.

> If you were born before the 1980s, like I was, you will remember the days
> when food was cooked in an oven. Long, laborious hours of waiting for
> the cry of 'dinner', when at last our exhausted mum would emerge from
> the steamy kitchen and scold us for not laying the table. This was only the
> 5 beginning of this drawn-out ritual. After we quickly devoured our plates of
> food, there was yet more waiting. Then we sat quietly at the table, whilst
> orders were taken for dessert. However, dessert was eaten very slowly as
> we all realised that washing up came next. Just as a reminder for those of
> you aged under 20, in those days a 'dishwasher' was me with a sponge
> 10 and my brother with a tea towel.
>
> The waiting time before dinner was often filled with watching whatever
> channel my father had decided on (there were only three) on the giant,
> monstrous television set, whilst bickering with my sibling over who got
> to sit in the comfy chair/stroke the dog/read the TV guide. This ended
> 15 sooner rather than later in a full-on fight with one of us on the floor and
> dad shouting at us to go out and play. Such happy domesticity.
>
> Online food blog

1. Choose four statements below which are true.

A The writer always ate all her food quickly, especially dessert.

B The writer thinks that food is no longer cooked in the oven.

C The writer always remembered to lay the table.

D The writer ate her dessert slowly as she was not hungry.

E The writer likes to wash up.

F The writer was not allowed to choose which TV channel to watch.

G The writer and her brother always argued whilst waiting for dinner.

H The writer and her brother annoyed their father as he watched TV.

Note it!

You need to read each statement very carefully. As the example on page 6 shows, one word can make a big difference to the accuracy and meaning of a statement.

What will you be asked?

- **Question 2** is worth **8 marks**.
- It will ask you to **summarise** and **synthesise** information **from both sources** on the exam paper **in a single response.**
- You will need to **summarise information: identify key points** in a text **and rewrite them concisely**, in **your own words** as far as possible.
- You will also need to **synthesise information: combine ideas** or **details from different sources** to **make a new text.**

What should you look for?

- The question could ask you to **synthesise** the **similarities or differences** between the **content of the texts.**
- It will **not** ask you to **identify** or **analyse writer's methods.**

Putting it into practice

Read the practice question below.

2. You need to refer to **Source A** and **Source B** for this question. Both sources describe what people do before their dinner.

Use details from **both** sources. Write a summary of the different ways that people behave before their dinner.

How can you approach it?

- Read the question carefully and look for the key area that you will need to identify (highlighted yellow).
- Then check again to see if you need to find **similarities** or **differences** (highlighted green).
- Once you have identified what you need to summarise, reread both texts and locate or find any relevant ideas. Look at how these have been highlighted in Sources A and B on page 9.

Note it!

Carefully choose quotations that summarise the key ideas. Remember to use short quotations and then use your own words to explain further.

Source A

The waiting time before dinner was often filled with watching whatever channel my father had decided upon (there were only three) on the giant, monstrous television set, whilst bickering with my sibling over who got to sit in the comfy chair/stroke the dog/read the TV guide. This ended
5 *sooner rather than later in a full-on fight with one of us on the floor and dad shouting at us to go out and play. Such happy domesticity.*

Source B

*THE HALF-HOUR BEFORE DINNER has always been considered as the great ordeal through which the mistress, in giving a dinner-party, will either pass with flying colours, or, lose many of her **laurels**. The anxiety to receive her guests, – her hope that all will be present in due time, – her trust in*
5 *the skill of her cook, and the attention of the other domestics, all tend to make these few minutes a trying time. The mistress, however, must display no kind of agitation, but show her tact in suggesting light and cheerful subjects of conversation, which will be much aided by the introduction of any particular new book, curiosity of art, or **article of vertu**, which may*
10 *pleasantly engage the attention of the company.*

From *The Book of Household Management* by Mrs Beeton

Glossary

laurels honour or distinction

article of vertu rare or beautiful object

- When you have identified relevant ideas from both texts, you will need to pull these ideas together to make your summary.

As you practise these skills, you might wish to use a table like this to help you plan your answer.

	Source A	Source B
Part 1	• The writer sounds frustrated: 'whatever channel my father had decided upon'. • She may be bored, and ends up 'bickering' with her sibling. • She does not seem to care about how those around her feel.	• It seems like the mistress is being tested/judged by others. • She feels 'the great ordeal', 'anxiety'. • She has to rely on the skills of others.
Part 2	• The situation worsens and ends in a 'full-on fight' and 'dad shouting'. • The writer seems sarcastic when she uses the word 'happy'.	• She has to pretend that she is calm. • She 'must display no kind of agitation', but have 'tact' and 'light' and cheerful' subjects of conversation.

- Focus on explaining the different ways that people behave before dinner that you have identified, using one piece of evidence from each text. You do not need to include a wide range of examples to make the same point.

Note it!

Remember that this is an 8-mark question. You should therefore aim to spend only 8–10 minutes on your answer. As you improve with practice, you will be able to work quickly from the texts without needing to use a table to plan.

Exam focus

How do I write up my summary?

Read this extract from a sample response.

The two extracts present the time before dinner as a difficult time, but in different ways. In Source A, the writer is frustrated as she is not allowed to do her own thing. She has to watch 'whatever channel my father had decided upon'. She also seems unhappy as she ends up 'bickering' with her sibling. The writer focuses on her feelings and does not seem concerned about the feelings of others, which is very different to Source B.

> Begins with a statement about both texts

> Makes inference about character's behaviour

> Embedded quotation

In contrast to this, although the writer of Source B also describes the time before dinner as very difficult, this is because of the 'anxiety' that it causes the person hosting the dinner as she is worried about impressing others. The dinner is described as 'the great ordeal' and it seems as if she is being tested or judged by others. This is not helped by the fact that she is not preparing the dinner herself, so she is relying on the skills of her servants to impress her visitors.

> Develops the point

> Links to Source B

What mistakes might you have made? (AO1)

- You might have identified or included analysis of the writer's methods, which is not necessary in this response.
- You might not have linked or compared the texts clearly.

Now you try!

Write the second part of the summary using the notes from your plan on page 10.

Remember:

- Use some linking **connectives**, e.g. 'On the other hand', 'Whereas', 'Unlike', 'In contrast', 'Moreover'.
- Focus on explaining ideas from the texts in your own words.
- Keep your quotations as short as possible.

How can you quote or paraphrase effectively?

- In exam **questions 2, 3 and 4,** you will need to use evidence from the text to support your comments. You can do this by either:
  quoting – using the exact words used, in quotation marks
  or
  paraphrasing – putting the information into your own words.
- You should aim to **use a balance between quoting and paraphrasing** in your responses.

Putting it into practice

Read the extract below. Then read the example language analysis for Question 3.

> **3.** How does the writer use language to show the discomfort of the dinner hostess?

You will need to:

- select appropriate quotations (usually a word, phrase or shorter part of a sentence)

- analyse the quotation or aspects of it.

THE HALF-HOUR BEFORE DINNER has always been considered as the great ordeal through which the mistress, in giving a dinner-party, will either pass with flying colours, or, lose many of her laurels. The anxiety to receive her guests – her hope that all will be present in due time, – her trust in the skill of her cook, and the attention of the other domestics, all tend to make these few minutes a trying time.

This use of hyperbole allows you to analyse the hostess's anxiety.

This contrast between passing and failing offers a good chance to analyse the imagery.

The connotations of these abstract nouns can be analysed to explore the feelings of the hostess.

Note it!

Try to use some direct quotation in your language analysis and always choose short quotations. These show the examiner that you are able to select evidence in a precise way.

Exam focus

How do I write up my language analysis?

Read through the two student responses below which show the alternative ways of using evidence.

Quoting

The writer uses language to show the discomfort of the hostess in Source B. The description of the dinner as 'the great ordeal' uses hyperbole to exaggerate her suffering. The word 'great' creates a sense of how huge her suffering is and the word 'ordeal' compares the hosting of dinner to a life or death challenge.

| Embedded quotation |
| Identification of literary technique |
| Analysis of language |

Paraphrasing

In Source B, the writer also describes the time before dinner as very difficult but this is because the person hosting the dinner is worried about impressing her guests and it all going to plan. The dinner is described almost as a matter of life or death and it seems as if she is being tested or judged by others.

| Describes what happens in the text without using direct quotations |
| Explains the character's feelings |
| Explains the writer's intention |

Now you try!

Write a sentence paraphrasing the ideas in the last sentence of the extract on page 12. Then write a sentence using direct quotations for the same line.

My progress Needs more work ☐ Getting there ☐ Sorted! ☐ **13**

What will you be asked?

- **Question 3** is worth **12 marks**.
- It asks you to **analyse language**.
- It could be **based on a specific part** of either **Source A or Source B**.
- You may also have to **explore how the text offers the writer's** viewpoint **or ideas**.

How would you answer this question?

A typical question might be:

> **3.** How does the writer use language to show the discomfort of the hostess?

First, **read the text closely**, underlining or **highlighting key words** or phrases that **relate to the focus of the question**.

Then **annotate** your chosen key words and phrases. Write down:

- the **meanings and** connotations
- **literary techniques**
- **effects of the words and phrases**
- the **link between your analysis** and the **question**.

Putting it into practice

Read the practice question below.

You now need to refer **only** to **Source A** from **lines 1 to 8**.

Q: How does the writer use language to show her frustration?

Now look at this sentence from the source (on page 7) to tackle the answer.

> *Long, laborious hours of waiting for the cry of 'dinner'; when at last our exhausted mum would emerge from the steamy kitchen and scold us for not laying the table.*

How can you approach it?

Read this analysis of the sentence using the approach on page 14.

- 'Long' implies an extended period of time; 'laborious' reinforces this and the amount of effort required; 'hours' also implies a long period of time, but could be **hyperbole**.
- Alliteration ('long, laborious') draws out the sound, emphasising the passing of time.
- Effect: this focus on the length of time shows the writer's frustration.
- Link to question: the writer is showing what it feels like from a child's point of view.

Note it!

Be sure to explain the meanings or connotations of individual words and phrases before you explore their effects.

Exam focus

How do I analyse language effectively? AO2

Read this paragraph which shows how to analyse language effectively.

In this section the writer over-emphasises the passage of time to convey her frustration to the reader. The alliterative phrase 'long, laborious hours' does this, with both 'long' and 'laborious' repeating this idea of the passage of time. The use of 'hours' reinforces this as it makes us think that this has been an incredibly long time, as seen from a child's perspective. This hyperbole might imply the child is exaggerating her wait, but this contributes to a light-hearted tone – the writer looking back at her younger self, which may amuse the reader.

| Meanings or connotations of individual words and phrases |
| Use of literary techniques |
| Effect of the words/ phrases that you have identified |
| The link between explanation/analysis and the question |

Now you try!

Now use selected references from the extract below to write a short paragraph about how language reveals the writer's frustration.

> This was, however, only the beginning of this drawn out ritual. After we quickly devoured our plates of food there was yet more waiting. Then we sat quietly at the table, whilst orders were taken for dessert.

What will you be asked?

- **Question 4** is **worth 16 marks**.
- It asks you to **compare Sources A and B** in a **longer answer**.
- The **question** will focus on the **viewpoints and attitudes** in the two sources.
- It could ask you to look for **similarities or differences**.
- It usually asks you to look at **both sources in full**.
- You will be expected to explore and **compare writers' methods** in addition to their **viewpoints, attitudes** or **ideas**.

How should you plan your answer?

A typical question might be:

> 4. Compare how the two writers convey their different perspectives and feelings about dining with others.
> In your answer, you should:
>
> - compare their different **perspectives and feelings**
> - compare the **methods** they use to convey their perspectives and feelings
> - support your ideas with **quotations** from both texts.

You should spend 5 minutes planning your response before you begin writing.

- First, identify the writers' **different perspectives** and **feelings**.
- Re-read the sources and select *quotations as evidence* for the different perspectives and feelings.
- Note the methods the writer uses in each of the selected quotations.

Putting it into practice

Now read Sources A and B in full.

Source A

It's time to wake up and smell the gravy

If you were born before the 1980s, like I was, you will remember the days when food was cooked in an oven. Long, laborious hours of waiting for

---

the cry of 'dinner', when at last our exhausted mum would emerge from the steamy kitchen and scold us for not laying the table. This was only the
5 beginning of this drawn-out ritual. After we quickly devoured our plates of food, there was yet more waiting. Then we sat quietly at the table, whilst orders were taken for dessert. However, dessert was eaten very slowly as we all realised that washing up came next. Just as a reminder for those of you aged under 20, in those days a 'dishwasher' was me with a sponge and my
10 brother with a tea towel.

The waiting time before dinner was often filled with watching whatever channel my father had decided on (there were only three) on the giant, monstrous television set, whilst bickering with my sibling over who got to sit in the comfy chair/stroke the dog/read the TV guide. This ended sooner rather
15 than later in a full-on fight with one of us of the floor and dad shouting at us to go out and play. Such happy domesticity.

Fast forward to the 1980s and the arrival of what looked like a TV set for the kitchen. In those early days of 'micro chips' and microwave pizza, who knew that this appliance would revolutionise how a whole generation of people
20 viewed food. The microwave has now become a permanent fixture in most households, that familiar 'ping' encouraging you to speed up your life. Why wait? You can have your chips NOW! In 2017, 93% of households owned a microwave. With the decline in the purchase of fresh vegetables and the increasing popularity of takeaway food, we have become a nation that has
25 lost the ritual of eating together.

Does it matter? Think back to your own childhood – it is often the small moments, like helping with the washing up, that are your fondest memories. The more we speed up our lives, the more we fast forward over these moments. With millions of people living alone in the UK, we are creating a
30 culture where eating together has lost its importance; living alone and eating fast is the new norm.

So next time you are tempted to reach for a microwave meal, or the takeaway menu, think twice – it's time to slow down and smell the gravy (or argue over whose turn it is to make it).

Online food blog

Source B

THE HALF-HOUR BEFORE DINNER has always been considered as the great ordeal through which the mistress, in giving a dinner-party, will either pass with flying colours, or, lose many of her laurels. The anxiety to receive her guests, – her hope that all will be present in due time, – her trust in the skill of
5 her cook, and the attention of the other domestics, all tend to make these few minutes a trying time. The mistress, however, must display no kind of

agitation, but show her tact in suggesting light and cheerful subjects of conversation, which will be much aided by the introduction of any particular new book, curiosity of art, or article of vertu, which may pleasantly engage the
10 attention of the company. "Waiting for Dinner," however, is a trying time, and there are few who have not felt –

"How sad it is to sit and pine,
The long half-hour before we dine!
Upon our watches oft to look,
15 Then wonder at the clock and cook,
...

"And strive to laugh in spite of Fate!
But laughter forced soon quits the room,
And leaves it in its former gloom.
20 But lo! the dinner now appears,
The object of our hopes and fears,
The end of all our pain!"

In giving an entertainment of this kind, the mistress should remember that it is her duty to make her guests feel happy, comfortable, and quite at
25 their ease; and the guests should also consider that they have come to the house of their hostess to be happy.

From *The Book of Household Management* by Mrs Beeton

How can you approach it?

Completing a table like this may help you to plan your response.

	Source A		Source B	
	Perspectives/ feelings	Evidence/ methods	Perspectives/ feelings	Evidence/ methods
1	Begins with a negative tone, complaining about waiting to eat	• First person • 'long laborious hours' • 'ordeal'	Negative tone tells the hostess what to do and using the idea of a test or race to explain this	• Third person • 'great ordeal' • 'pass with flying colours' • 'trying time'
2	Seems frustrated; she can't choose TV programme and ends up fighting with her brother	• Alliteration of 'full-on fight' • Irony of 'happy domesticity'	The writer tells the hostess that she must not show her worries and stress	Modal verbs convey guidance: 'must'; 'should'; 'must display no kind of agitation'

- Aim to make **three or four detailed comparisons** for this question.
- The table shows the range of methods or evidence you could use for two comparisons. You won't need to use so many in the exam.

Now try and add two more comparisons to your table.

Exam focus

How do I write up my analysis? **AO3**

Read the extract below from a successful response comparing Sources A and B. It uses point 1 from the table.

Note it!

Remember, the methods you explore don't have to be just language points. You could also explore structure or consider other methods like tone, register and voice.

Both writers begin with very negative ideas about dining with others but from very different perspectives. Source A is written in the first person and gives a very personal view, which seems to be reflecting upon the experience of the writer as a child, about how it is an 'ordeal' to wait for dinner. The alliterative phrase 'long, laborious hours' reinforces this, with both 'long' and 'laborious' emphasising the passage of time and therefore her suffering.

In contrast, although Source B is also about how difficult it is to wait for dinner, it is written in the third person and seems more focused on giving advice to the hostess to prevent any bad experiences for the guests. It is presented as a test that she should hope to 'pass with flying colours' or she will lose her 'laurels'. The word 'laurels' is chosen to symbolise the respect and reward she will gain as a successful hostess. This reinforces the writer's viewpoint that the reader risks losing their status if they do not follow her advice.

> Point of comparison
>
> Textual evidence
>
> Analyses writer's methods
>
> Comments on contrasting voice

Now you try!

Using point 2 from the table on page 18, write your own comparison paragraphs.

1. Look at this ideas map representing the skill of summarising. Is there anything else you could add?

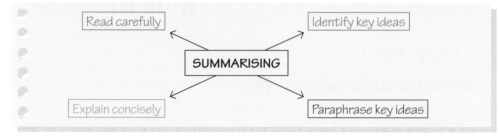

2. Create an ideas map for another reading skill you will need for the exam.

Quick quiz

Answer these questions about reading skills and the questions you will face.

1. How many statements do you have to identify as true for Question 1?
2. Do you have to look at a specific extract or the full text for Question 1?
3. What is a summary?
4. What is synthesis?
5. What four things should you do when quoting from a text?
6. What is the difference between quoting and paraphrasing?
7. For which question should you use paraphrasing because it asks you to describe or explain ideas?
8. For which questions should you use direct quotations as these questions ask you to analyse methods?
9. What does Question 3 ask you to analyse?
10. Do you have to look at an extract or the full text for Question 3?
11. Name three literary techniques that you might analyse for Question 3.
12. What is the main focus for Question 4?
13. What is viewpoint?
14. What methods can you use to support your comparisons in Question 4?
15. How long should you spend in planning your response to Question 4?

Practise your skills

Read the short extract below, then answer the practice task.

> *Riding became so important to me – it was like I was born to be with Meggy. Meggy was my first horse: my best friend, my companion and fellow adventurer. We could spend hours trekking through the hills; time passing in the blink of an eye. Riding made me feel so alive.*

Q: Which two of the following four statements are true?

A Riding is a very important part of the writer's life.

B Meggy was the writer's only horse.

C The writer likes to spend a long time riding her horse.

D The writer thinks that time passes slowly when she is out riding.

Power paragraphs

Read the extract below from an autobiography published in 1900 about sailing around the world. Then answer the following practice task.

> *About midnight the fog shut down again denser than ever before. One could almost 'stand on it'. It continued so for a number of days, the wind increasing to a gale. The waves rose high, but I had a good ship. Still, in the dismal fog I felt myself drifting into loneliness, an insect on a straw in the midst of the elements.*
>
> from *Sailing Alone Around the World* by Joshua Slocum

Q: How does the writer use language here to describe the effects of the weather?

Write a paragraph commenting on the writer's choice of **one** of the following:

- words and phrases
- language features and techniques
- sentence forms.

Five key things about Paper 2, Section A

1. Paper 2, Section A contains **four questions** based on **two sources**.
   - Source A will be from the twentieth or twenty-first century and Source B is likely to be from the nineteenth century. Both will express viewpoints in some way and be on related topics.
   - They could be in a range of non-fiction forms, such as magazine articles, news stories, letters or journals.
2. The **questions** in Section A are worth **a total of 40 marks** (half the marks for Paper 2).
3. You will have **60 minutes** to read the extract and answer the questions, **including up to 15 minutes for reading**.
4. You may find it helpful to **read the extracts once**, then **read the questions**, then reread and **annotate the extracts**.
5. There are **no marks** for spelling, punctuation or grammar in Paper 2, Section A. However, if you **express yourself clearly and accurately** it will be easier for the examiner to **understand your answers and credit you for them**.

What skills will each question test?

The table below provides an overview of what each of the four reading questions in Section A involves. It also shows the marks allocated to each one.

Question	Marks	What you must do
1	4	**Choose true statements** from a list of statements (some of which are untrue) and **shade in the boxes** to indicate your answers.
2	8	**Summarise and synthesise differences or similarities** between the **two sources**.
3	12	**Analyse** in detail the **language** in **one** of the two sources.
4	16	**Compare how** the writers of **both sources convey their viewpoints and attitudes** (by the methods they use).

For **Question 1**, you simply have to identify the correct statements. For **Questions 2 and 4**, you have to compare the two texts, using evidence from the text, and including analysis for **Question 4**. For **Question 3**, you also need to support your ideas and understanding with evidence and analysis.

What do you need to do to get a good mark?

Use this grid to understand what your current level is and how to improve it.

	AO1 **(Q1 and Q2) Identify and interpret Select and synthesise**	AO2 **(Q3) Explain, comment on, and analyse language and structure**	AO4 **(Q4) Compare ideas and perspectives**
High	• You accurately **identify key points** • You make **perceptive inference** and interpretations from **both texts** • You use textual detail in a **well-judged way**	• You **analyse** the writer's choice of **language** • You make **sophisticated and accurate** use of **subject terminology** • You select textual evidence in a **well-judged way**	• You **compare and analyse** ideas and methods in a **perceptive** way • You show a **detailed understanding** of the ideas in **both texts** • You select evidence from **both texts** in a **well-judged way**
Mid	• You identify **most key points** • You make **clear inferences** and identify differences • You use **relevant textual detail** to support your points	• You **explain clearly** the effects of the writer's choice of language • You use **subject terminology** in a **clear and accurate** way • You select a range of **relevant textual detail**	• You **compare and explain** ideas and methods in a **clear** way • You show **a clear understanding** of the ideas in **both texts** • You select **relevant detail** from **both texts**
Lower	• You identify **some key points** • You make some **basic inferences** • You use **some relevant textual details** to support your points	• You make **simple comments** on the effects of language • You make **simple use** of **subject terminology, not always accurately** • You select **simple textual details** to support your points	• You make **simple reference** to ideas and methods from both texts • You show **simple awareness** of different ideas in the texts • You select **simple textual details** from **one or both** texts

Read these two sample reading extracts

Source A

This extract is taken from an article published by Greg Ray in the Newcastle Herald *in Australia after he interviewed a famous yachtsman. He describes his concerns about the damage caused to the ocean by humans through overfishing and pollution.*

> **The Ocean is Broken**
> **Greg Ray**
> It was the silence that made this voyage different from all of those before it.
> Not the absence of sound, exactly. The wind still whipped the sails and
> whistled in the rigging. The waves still sloshed against the fibreglass hull.
> And there were plenty of other noises: muffled thuds and bumps and scrapes
> 5   as the boat knocked against pieces of debris. What was missing was the cries of
> the seabirds which, on all previous similar voyages, had surrounded the boat.
> The birds were missing because the fish were missing. Exactly 10 years before,
> when Newcastle yachtsman Ivan Macfadyen had sailed exactly the same course
> from Melbourne to Osaka, all he'd had to do to catch a fish from the ocean
> 10   between Brisbane and Japan was throw out a baited line.
> "There was not one of the 28 days on that portion of the trip when we didn't
> catch a good-sized fish to cook up and eat with some rice," Macfadyen recalled.
> But this time, on that whole long leg of sea journey, the total catch was two. No
> fish. No birds. Hardly a sign of life at all.
> 15   "In years gone by I'd gotten used to all the birds and their noises," he said.
> "They'd be following the boat, sometimes resting on the mast before taking
> off again. You'd see flocks of them wheeling over the surface of the sea in the
> distance, feeding on pilchards."
> But in March and April this year, only silence and desolation surrounded
> 20   his boat, *Funnel Web*, as it sped across the surface of a haunted ocean. If that
> sounds depressing, it only got worse. The next leg of the long voyage was from
> Osaka to San Francisco and for most of that trip the desolation was tinged with
> nauseous horror and a degree of fear.
> "After we left Japan, it felt as if the ocean itself was dead," Macfadyen said. "We
> 25   hardly saw any living things. We saw one whale, sort of rolling helplessly on the
> surface with what looked like a big tumour on its head. It was pretty sickening.
> I've done a lot of miles on the ocean in my life and I'm used to seeing turtles,

dolphins, sharks and big flurries of feeding birds. But this time, for 3000 nautical miles there was nothing alive to be seen."

30 In place of the missing life was garbage in astounding volumes. Ivan's brother, Glenn, who boarded at Hawaii for the run into the United States, marvelled at the "thousands on thousands" of yellow plastic buoys. The huge tangles of synthetic rope, fishing lines and nets. Pieces of polystyrene foam by the million. And slicks of oil and petrol, everywhere. Countless hundreds of

35 wooden power poles are out there, snapped off by the killer wave and still trailing their wires in the middle of the sea.

'In years gone by, when you were becalmed by lack of wind, you'd just start your engine and motor on,' Ivan said.

Not this time.

40 'In a lot of places we couldn't start our motor for fear of entangling the propeller in the mass of pieces of rope and cable. That's an unheard of situation, out in the ocean.

'If we did decide to motor we couldn't do it at night, only in the daytime with a lookout on the bow, watching for rubbish.

45 'On the bow, in the waters above Hawaii, you could see right down into the depths. I could see that the debris isn't just on the surface, it's all the way down. And it's all sizes, from a soft-drink bottle to pieces the size of a big car or truck.

'We saw a factory chimney sticking out of the water, with some kind of boiler thing still attached below the surface. We saw a big container-type thing, just

50 rolling over and over on the waves.

'We were weaving around these pieces of debris. It was like sailing through a garbage tip.

'Below decks you were constantly hearing things hitting against the hull, and you were constantly afraid of hitting something really big. As it was, the hull

55 was scratched and dented all over the place from bits and pieces we never saw.'

Plastic was ubiquitous. Bottles, bags and every kind of throwaway domestic item you can imagine, from broken chairs to dustpans, toys and utensils.

And something else. The boat's vivid yellow paint job, never faded by sun or sea in years gone past, reacted with something in the water off Japan, losing its

60 sheen in a strange and unprecedented way.

Back in Newcastle, Ivan Macfadyen is still coming to terms with the shock and horror of the voyage.

'The ocean is broken,' he said,

65 shaking his head in stunned disbelief.

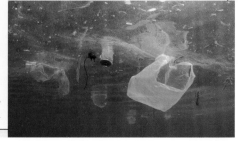

Newcastle Herald, October 13,

www.theherald.com.au

Source B

This is an extract from South! *which was written by Ernest Shackleton, first published in 1919. It is an autobiographical account of his journey on the ship* Endurance *to try and reach the South Pole.*

Into the Weddell Sea

The situation became dangerous that night. We pushed into the **pack** in the hope of reaching open water beyond, and found ourselves after dark in a pool which was growing smaller and smaller. The ice was grinding around the ship in the heavy swell, and I watched with some anxiety for any indication of a
5 change of wind to the east, since a breeze from that quarter would have driven us towards the land. Worsley and I were on deck all night, dodging the pack. At 3 a.m. we ran south, taking advantage of some openings that had appeared, but met heavy rafted pack-ice, evidently old; some of it had been subjected to severe pressure. Then we stormed north-west and saw open water to the north-
10 east. I put the *Endurance*'s head for the opening, and, steaming at full speed, we got clear. Then we went east in the hope of getting better ice, and five hours later, after some dodging, we rounded the pack and were able to set sail once more. This initial tussle with the pack had been exciting at times.

Pieces of ice and bergs of all sizes were heaving and jostling against each other
15 in the heavy south-westerly swell. In spite of all our care the *Endurance* struck large lumps stem on, but the engines were stopped in time and no harm was done. The scene and sounds through the day were very fine. The swell was dashing against the sides of huge bergs and leaping right to the top of their icy cliffs. Sanders Island lay to the south, with a few rocky faces peering through
20 the misty, swirling clouds that swathed it most of the time, the booming of the sea running into ice-caverns, the swishing break of the swell on the loose pack, and the graceful blowing and undulating of the inner pack to the steeply rolling swell, which here was robbed of its break by the masses of ice to windward.

Glossary

pack large pieces of floating ice driven together into one large mass, as often seen in polar seas

Next read these sample exam questions

Section A: Reading

1. Reread the first section of **Source A** from **lines 1 to 16**.

   Choose **four** statements below which are TRUE.

   A There is no noise at all on the voyage.

   B The yachtsman noticed the lack of noise from the seabirds.

   C Both the writer and the yatchsman are shocked by the lack of fish and birds.

   D The birds were missing because it is too far to fly.

   E The yachtsman has sailed the course before.

   F The yachtsman is finding it difficult to fish because he is out of practice.

   G On his previous trip he didn't catch any decent sized fish to eat.

   H On this leg of the journey, the yachtsman has only caught two fish.

   [4 marks]

2. You need to refer to **Source A** and **Source B** for this question.

   The way that the writers describe the ocean is very different.

   Use the details from **both** sources. Write a summary of the different descriptions of the ocean. **[8 marks]**

3. You now need to refer **only** to **Source B**, **lines 1–13**.

   How does the writer use language to describe the danger that the ship faces? **[12 marks]**

4. For this question, you need to refer to the **whole of Source A**, together with the **whole of Source B**.

   Compare how the two writers convey their different perspectives and feelings about the ocean.

   In your answer, you could:

   - compare their different perspectives and feelings on the ocean
   - compare the methods the writers use to convey their perspectives and feelings
   - support your response with references to both texts. **[16 marks]**

Now reread the questions and consider these sample answers

1. The four true answers are:

B. The yatchsman noticed the lack of noise from the seabirds.

C. Both the writer and the yatchsman are shocked by the lack of fish and birds.

E. The yatchsman has sailed the course before.

H. On this leg of the journey, the yatchsman has only caught two fish.

2.

Both writers describe the power of the ocean but in very different ways. In Source A the writer describes the ocean as silent, with the only noises created by man-made things, the 'muffled thuds and bumps' as the boat is hit by debris in the ocean. This silence presents the ocean as if it has lost its power, because of the actions of humanity.

In contrast to this Source B describes the ocean as a powerful force of nature. The ice grinds against the ship and the swell of waves is described as 'heavy'. Shackleton describes the boat as 'dodging' and tussling with the ice; the boat is fighting the ice which makes the ocean sound very powerful against this man-made object. He also seems to describe the ocean as a place of excitement and wonder, even though it is clearly very dangerous, which contrasts with Source A. He describes his journey through the ice as 'exciting at times' and he considers what he can see and hear as 'very fine'.

However, Source A presents the ocean as 'haunted', a place of 'desolation' because of the lack of sea life and because of the obvious debris caused by humans. Any beauty the ocean may have had has been destroyed by 'garbage in astounding volumes'. So the ocean is presented as a 'sickening' place that makes the writer, and the reader, feel horrified.

3.

The writer of Source B relays the danger that he faces by first describing the power of the ice pack. The repetition of the comparative adjective 'smaller' suggests that the ship is trapped by the ice closing in and makes the reader feel that there is no escape. This is further reinforced by the description of the ice 'grinding' against the ship. This conveys to the reader a harsh and grating noise which might suggest that the hull is being damaged and justifies the writer's implied anxiety, creating a sense of danger and threat.

In addition to this, the writer then goes on to personify the ship using a range of verbs that suggest that the ship is both battling the ice and trying to escape from it. The use of the verbs 'dodging' and 'ran' both imply possible escape, personifying the ship as if it is desperate to ensure that it gets away from the ice. The use of the verbs 'stormed' and 'steaming' portray more physically aggressive actions, implying that the ship is actively fighting against the ice.

Note it!

Remember that you can re-use ideas and analysis from your response to Question 3 in your response to Question 4.

4.

Both writers have very different perspectives towards the ocean. In Source A the writer clearly admires and respects the ocean but is upset by the way it has been harmed by humans. Source A uses stark juxtapositions to show the destruction that has been caused to the ocean and its effect on the writer. First, the reference to 'silence' in line 1 juxtaposes with the alliterative description of the wind as it 'whipped' and 'whistled' in line 3. This image of nature is further reinforced by the onomatopoeia used to describe the waves as they 'still sloshed' against the boat. Both of these images create a sense of the beauty of nature and the writer's admiration for these things, which emphasises the upsetting nature of the damage to the ocean caused by humans. A further use of onomatopoeia with the 'muffled thuds and bumps' against the boat reveals the unnatural sounds created by human debris, contrasting with the effect of the first use of this technique.

Source B also shows the beauty and power of nature. The writer clearly respects the ocean, but he also sees it as a mighty force to be conquered or beaten. He suggests its beauty and power through his use of onomatopoeia, describing the ocean and the ice as 'booming' and 'swishing'. Both of these verbs remind the reader of the sounds of the sea, conveying the strength of the waves. Through the personification of the ocean as 'leaping' to the top of the 'icy cliffs' of the iceberg, the writer gives a sense that the ocean is so athletic it can reach any height.

In contrast to Source A, the writer of Source B shows an emotional reaction to the ocean but it is one of both fear and a wish to conquer and beat this powerful force. He conveys this attitude through his personification of the ship, using a range of verbs that suggest that the ship is both battling the ice and trying to escape from it. The use of the verbs 'dodging' and 'ran' both imply to the reader that the ship may be able to escape, with the verbs 'stormed' and 'steaming' suggesting that the ship is fighting against the ice more aggressively. The personification effectively reveals the writer's fear, but it also shows the reader how he seems determined to conquer the ice and sea. This is further emphasised by the use of the word 'tussle', which suggests a fight or scuffle between two people, but seems to trivialise how difficult the battle has been. By adopting this attitude, it is as if Shackleton is portraying his confidence and determination to win against the ice.

BASIC WRITING SKILLS
Varying sentence types

What will you have to do?

- **Question 5** is worth **40 marks**.
- It will ask you to focus on effectively expressing your viewpoint.
- You should **use a variety of sentence types** and **lengths** to achieve a **range of effects** in your writing.

How can you identify the three main sentence types?

- The **three main types of sentence** are **simple**, **compound** and **complex**.
- Use the table below to remind yourself how the **three different sentence types** are **constructed**.

Types	Definition	Examples
Simple	Simple sentences contain a subject and a verb. Sometimes they also contain an object.	*I work online.* *I can research any topic.*
Compound	Compound sentences join two simple sentences using a coordinating conjunction, such as 'and', 'but', 'or', 'nor', 'so' or 'yet'.	*Reading is an important skill and everyone should learn to read.* *Reading is important, so schools should make sure that students can access books.*
Complex	Complex sentences include a main clause that makes sense on its own and at least one subordinate clause that only makes sense in relation to the main clause.	*Ellis, although he has never really been an avid reader, has consumed all of the Harry Potter books.* *Having revised all the poems, the students should be able to complete their poetry paper with ease.* *Reading, which is a very important skill, should not be tested in exams if we want students to enjoy it.*

Putting it into practice

Read the annotated extract from a student response below. Then consider how this student has used the different sentence types to express their view.

> Reading is an essential life skill. While some would argue we can access learning in other ways, researchers agree that reading is still central to children's development.

Simple sentence stating the writer's argument

Subordinate clause in this complex sentence states the counter-argument

Counter-argument rejected in the main clause

Exam focus

How do I use a range of sentence types? AO5 AO6

Consider how this extract from a student response is different from the one above.

Note it!

Simple sentences often work well at the beginning or end of a paragraph as they introduce and sum up key points concisely.

> Another point about reading is that it is not popular with young people anymore because they would rather be on social media than reading a book. You might disagree. You might think reading is fun. But most people don't. One survey suggested that only 40% of secondary-age students read in their spare time now and another survey suggested that borrowing books from libraries has fallen by 30%. This proves that reading is no longer a popular pastime.

What mistakes might you have made here?

- Beginning with a long, complex sentence might risk losing the reader's interest.
- Using a series of very short sentences together can sound too repetitive.
- Using a compound sentence to link two ideas that don't belong together weakens the points. These would be better as separate, more developed, complex sentences.

Now you try!

Rewrite the extract above to express the view more clearly. Use the advice on mistakes to help you vary the use of sentences.

My progress Needs more work ☐ Getting there ☐ Sorted! ☐   31

BASIC WRITING SKILLS
Using sentences for different purposes

What sentence types could you use?

● Aim to use a range of these different sentence types in your writing for **Question 5**.

Type	Purpose	Examples
Declarative sentences	Make a statement about someone or something. Most sentences are declarative.	*Neglect can cause animals to suffer in a range of different situations.*
Interrogative sentences	Request information and end with a question mark.	*Can't you see how animals are suffering?*
Exclamatory sentences	Show strong feelings and end with an exclamation mark.	*Animals are being tortured!*
Imperative sentences	Give a command in which the subject (second person 'you', singular or plural) is usually left out.	*Stop animals suffering.* (*You should stop animals suffering.*)

What sentence types suit different parts of viewpoint essays?

● It is unlikely you would start a viewpoint essay with an exclamation. More likely is a statement in which you introduce the issue. For example, *The use of plastics is a real scourge on our oceans.*
● Interrogative sentences in the form of **rhetorical questions** usually come further into the argument, perhaps to emphasise a point you have made. For example: *Can we really let this situation continue?*
● You should not always end a viewpoint essay like this but sometimes an imperative sentence would be a good way of hammering home a final point or providing a call to action. For example: *Act now to avoid a catastrophe in our forests.*

What verb tense is it best to use?

- For **Question 5** you will mainly **write in the present tense**, especially in forms like a speech or a letter. For example: I *believe we are damaging* the environment...
- Writing in the **present tense** can create a **sense of immediacy**; making a clear **connection with the reader**. For example: *Don't you agree?*
- The **past tense** can be needed for anecdotes or to report past events relevant to the topic. For example: *Yesterday, vehicle fumes really affected me...*

How do you use verb tenses and modals correctly?

- **Many verbs** follow **similar spelling patterns** when they **change tenses** or **shift from singular to plural**. For example:
  - **Simple present tense:** 'I help', 'you help', 'he/she/it help**s**'.
  - **Simple past tense:** 'I help**ed**', 'you help**ed**', 'he/she/it help**ed**'.
- **Modal verbs modify verbs** to indicate **certainty**, **obligation** or **possibility**. Use them to **reinforce your attitude**, viewpoint or to instruct to the reader.

Note it!

Be aware that modals expressing possibility (such as 'might') can be very useful when interpreting ideas in literature texts (or in Paper 1 Reading questions). For example: *The poet might be expressing his sadness about his son going to school for the first time.*

Purpose	Modal verbs	Examples
Certainty	will, won't, can, can't	*You can help save the whales.*
Obligation	have to, must, should	*You should consider how you could increase the amount of paper that you recycle.*
Possibility	may, might, could	*You could help to save the whales, if you contribute further to our campaign.*

33

Putting it into practice

Read these two statements and decide which student uses the better style for viewpoint writing.

> The cost of travel on public transport is ridiculous. Young people need to travel cheaply; their fares should be subsidised until they leave education.

> The cost of travel on public transport was ridiculous. Young people needed to travel cheaply; their fares should have been subsidised until they left education.

Putting it into practice

Rewrite each of the following three sentences in a different modal form, as shown in brackets.

- A reduction in plastics use might be achieved by using recyclable paper for fruit and vegetables. (change to **certainty**)
- People will be resistant to change. (change to **possibility**)
- People will change their habits if they want a better environment. (change to **obligation**)

Note it!

You could also use the simple future tense to indicate what you want to happen next. For example: *We will make sure that no more animals suffer in this way.*

Exam focus

How do I use modal verbs in my writing?

Read the paragraph below and look at where the student uses modal verbs.

> It must be time to ban animal experiments. They are cruel and hurtful; why should animals suffer on our behalf? The phrase 'man's best friend' might often be used to refer to animals but is this the right way to treat a friend? Every year, hundreds of animals die needlessly in research labs. We can surely do something to help.

Reinforces to the reader that change needs to happen

Questions whether this practice is fair

Suggests possibility so that the reader is encouraged to consider this idea

Expresses certainty in the viewpoint

Now you try!

Rewrite and improve this viewpoint paragraph to give it greater impact. Focus on changing verb tenses and modal verbs.

> There could have been higher discounts on coach and train tickets for students. This would have increased the number of people using public transport so will be good for the environment. This has been the policy in other countries and so could have been done here. We could campaign for this and make a difference.

BASIC WRITING SKILLS
Using punctuation and forms of speech

How can you use punctuation for clarity and impact?

- **Persuasive sentences** can be even **more effective** if you **use a range of punctuation well**.
- You can use **punctuation** to **improve the clarity** of your writing, give **balance to your argument**, **emphasise specific points** or **create interest** for the reader.

What punctuation should you use in your writing?

In addition to full stops, try to use these forms of punctuation in your writing.

Punctuation	Purpose	Examples
Commas	• Separate the main clause in a sentence from the subordinate clause • Separate items in a list or a series of descriptions or to add clarity to a tricolon	*Pets, of all shapes and sizes, are adorable.* *Cats are a great pet; they give companionship, love and affection.*
Colons	• Indicate a pause or introduce a list in a sentence • The clause before the colon is a main clause and can stand on its own	*I have one favourite hobby in the whole world: dog walking.*
Semicolons	• Link two ideas, events or pieces of information • Also separate items in a long list	*Horse riding is important to me; it gives me the confidence to take risks.*
Dashes	• Separate parts of a sentence, but are mainly used for emphasis or additional explanation	*Dogs are so friendly – even large ones – and they really are man's best friend.*
Brackets	• Mark off extra information without altering the meaning of the sentence	*I have ridden horses (or ponies) since I was very young.*

How can you use reported speech in viewpoint writing?

- **Reported speech** is an account of what someone has said. It does not show the actual words spoken in speech marks. For example:

> Mr Hoyle, a well-renowned expert on pets, described how important they are. He explained that pet owners are 50% happier than non-pet owners and are 20% less likely to suffer from issues with their health.

- Reported speech is used in viewpoint writing to give the opinions of experts, as shown above, or when you are retelling an anecdote.
- Remember to use the past tense – you are reporting what has already been said.

How can you use direct speech in viewpoint writing?

- **Direct speech** is when you include a quotation of what someone has said in your writing. In viewpoint writing, you can use it to introduce the ideas or opinions of others, e.g. witnesses or experts.
- You can use it to add emphasis or importance to a particular statement to support your viewpoint. For example:

> Many experts promote the great benefits of having a pet. When interviewed, Mr Hoyle, a well-renowned expert on pets, stated 'Pets can have a significant impact on health and wellbeing. The results of my research show this unequivocally. We found that pet owners are 50% happier than non-pet owners.' It seems, therefore, that pets have the power to change lives for the better.

- Make the quotation well focused, place single inverted commas ('...') around it, and, if you can, embed your quotation into the sentence.

Note it!

Both direct speech and reported speech can add evidence to make an argument more persuasive. Direct speech draws the reader's attention to the individual view expressed and therefore gives the 'expert' more influence. Reported speech is more suitable for expressing general concerns, supporting other points you have made.

Putting it into practice

Look at how punctuation and direct/reported speech have been used to establish viewpoint in the paragraph below.

Many pet owners think that their pets are more important than humans; I do too! Owning a pet is an expensive business, especially in the UK, which some might argue is a waste of money. Some dog owners – of which I am one – treat their dogs like royalty: lavishing gifts upon them, taking them for doggy spa treatments and only buying the most expensive food. The views of the pet owners interviewed reinforced how important pets are as a companion. Fred, a dog owner from Derbyshire, stated 'My dog is my constant companion and without him I would be very lonely.'

Semicolon reinforces the writer's personal viewpoint.

Subordinate clause, separated by a pair of commas, gives greater detail, adding credibility to the argument.

Extra information within dashes reminds the reader of the writer's viewpoint.

Colon introduces list of activities.

Reported speech introduces evidence to make the argument sound convincing.

Direct speech appeals to the reader's emotions through the speaker's own words.

How can you approach it?

Think about the use of:

- a colon or semicolon to expand on a viewpoint
- commas and dashes to add extra information.

Note it!

You can also use a single dash in a similar way to a colon – to point to the importance of the information that follows after it in the second part of the sentence.

Exam focus

How do I use a range of punctuation in my writing? AO6

Read the student response below to see how you can use a range of punctuation.

Animals are such an important part of our lives, even though they are just pets. There are so many compelling reasons to get a pet: they are good company if you are lonely, they teach children to look after others and show compassion, and if you get a dog, it will encourage you to exercise! My grandmother has owned a poodle for many years (and a snooty Persian cat!) and told me she can't imagine living without them.

Comma to indicate subordinate clause

Colon to introduce list; commas to separate items in the list

Round brackets to give additional (humorous) information

Note it!

Semicolons and colons are easily confused. Use a semicolon to link two clauses together. Use a colon to focus the reader on what follows – a list or a quotation, for example.

Now you try!

Write a paragraph putting forward the counter-argument – that having a pet is overrated. Try to use:

- reported speech
- commas or dashes to separate subordinate clauses
- a colon or semicolon.

Why are paragraphs important?

- **Paragraphs** give **shape and structure** to your writing.
- They **help the reader to follow your ideas** and understand how they link together.
- A **new paragraph** indicates a **change of idea, topic, place** or **time**.
- When planning your answer to **Question 5**, make sure you organise your ideas into a clear sequence of paragraphs.

How can connectives help your writing?

- You can also use **connectives** to join your ideas together clearly.
- The table below reminds you of some common connectives and how to use them.

Addition of ideas	Order or sequence	Examples	Cause and effect
In addition	Firstly	For example	Consequently
As well as	Secondly	For instance	As a result
Besides	Next	Such as	Since
Also	Later	As can be seen	Because

Compare and contrast	Qualify	Purpose	Sum up
Similarly	However	To this end	Finally
In the same way	Still	For this purpose	To sum up
In contrast	Yet	For this reason	In conclusion
On the other hand	Having said that	In order to	

Putting it into practice

Read this practice question. Then look at page 41 to see how a student has used a spider diagram to order their paragraphs. Note their inclusion of connectives, too.

5. 'Exams are out of date and do not measure the skills that students need to be successful in the modern world.'

   Write a speech to be delivered to your headteacher in which you argue for or against this statement.

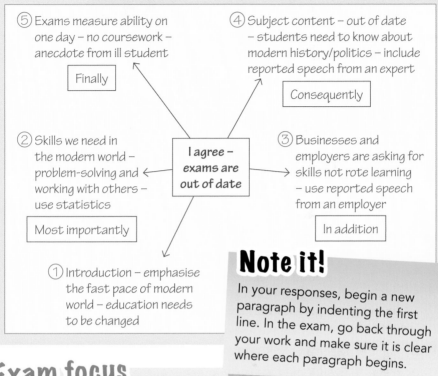

⑤ Exams measure ability on one day – no coursework – anecdote from ill student

Finally

④ Subject content – out of date – students need to know about modern history/politics – include reported speech from an expert

Consequently

② Skills we need in the modern world – problem-solving and working with others – use statistics

I agree – exams are out of date

③ Businesses and employers are asking for skills not rote learning – use reported speech from an employer

Most importantly

In addition

① Introduction – emphasise the fast pace of modern world – education needs to be changed

Note it!

In your responses, begin a new paragraph by indenting the first line. In the exam, go back through your work and make sure it is clear where each paragraph begins.

Exam focus

How do I use paragraphs and connectives in my writing? AO5 AO6

Read the beginning of this response, which uses the plan above.

The modern world we live in alters by the second, minute, hour. To achieve in this fast-paced world, students need the right skills; skills not currently provided by the education system and certainly not demonstrated in exams.

Most importantly, our education should provide us with the skills for success. What are they? Increasingly, society is realising that competent communication, problem-solving and showing initiative are the skills that make students successful in the modern world. Such abilities are rarely measured in the controlled world of an exam. In a recent survey, 80% of 18 year-olds said that they did not feel ready for their next step after A Level courses. We need change and fast.

Now you try!

Write the next paragraph to this response, following the diagram above.

My progress Needs more work ☐ Getting there ☐ Sorted! ☐ 41

BASIC WRITING SKILLS Spelling

Why is spelling important?

- **Spelling** is **important** because it improves the clarity of your writing and contributes to your mark for technical accuracy in **Question 5**.
- You can **improve your spelling** by learning spelling patterns and by keeping a **record** of the **mistakes you make**.

How can you reduce common spelling mistakes?

- Note down the tricky parts of spellings like this to help remember them:

Correct word	Reminder	Correct word	Reminder
ultimately	tim	*principle*	cip

- **Split complex words** into **sound sections** to help you visualise the spelling. Say each word **out loud** to hear **its rhythm** to help you remember, like this: *con-se-que-nt-ly   ar-gu-ment   com-plet-e   def-in-ite-ly*
- Use mnemonics – **phrases that act as memory aids**. Try creating a **nonsense phrase**, like the ones below, to remind you **how to spell a word**.

Word	Mnemonic
exaggerate	*Even X-men are going greener at the end.*
persuade	*Pink elephants regularly see umbrellas and dangly earrings.*

- Make up a **rhyme** to help you remember the hard part of a spelling:

Word	Rhyme reminder
separate	*There is **a rat** in sep**a**r**a**te.*
accommodation	*A good hotel always has two **c**hairs and two **m**attresses (two 'c's and two 'm's).*

What spellings should you learn?

Homophones

It is easy to make mistakes with common homophones like the ones below. So make up rhymes or mnemonics to help you learn them.

- **its** = shows belonging; **it's** = shortened form of 'it is'
- **their** = belongs to them; **there** = that place; **they're** = short for 'they are'
- **whose** = belonging to someone; **who's** = shortened form of 'who is'.

Plurals

- When you add 's' to nouns that end in 'y', change 'y' to 'ie' when there is a consonant before the 'y'. For example: *story – stories*.
- If there is a vowel before the 'y', just add 's': *monkey – monkeys*.
- Add 'es' to nouns that end in '-ch', '-s', '-sh', '-x', '-z': *beach – beaches*.
- Nouns ending in 'f' or 'fe' often change to 'v' when 'es' is added: *leaf – leaves*.
- For most nouns that end in 'ff' or have two vowels before 'f', just add 's': *puffs, reefs*.

Prefixes and suffixes

- Prefixes that end in a vowel do not change when added to a word. For example: *semi – semicircle; pre – premeditate*. However, double letters can occur: *mis – mi**ss**pell; ir – i**rr**egular*.
- When you add a suffix starting with a vowel to a word ending in a silent 'e', you usually drop the 'e': *adventure – adventur**ous**; excite – excit**able***. If the word ends in 'ce' or 'ge', you keep the 'e': *manage – manag**e**able*.
- When you add 'all', 'full' or 'till' to a word, drop the second 'l': *all – also, always; full – hopeful, fulfill; till – until*.

Putting it into practice

One student learned the differences between *there, their* and *they're* like this.

Word	Reminder
their	*When they read **their** books, **e**ven Iris reads.*
there	*Can you see **that** elephant over **there**? Elephants read **e**verything.*
they're	***They're** going to the gym later; **Y**asmin (apostrophe) **r**uns **e**xcellently.*

Note it!

A common mistake is to add the wrong prefix or suffix. If you are unsure, check in a dictionary and add it to your spelling bank.

Now you try!

Practise your skills by correcting the spelling mistakes in this paragraph.

Rats can make great pets as there very sociable and friendley. As long as you are mindfull that rats love climing and jumping, they are managable. They seem to be missunderstood by many familys and its an unnfair situation.

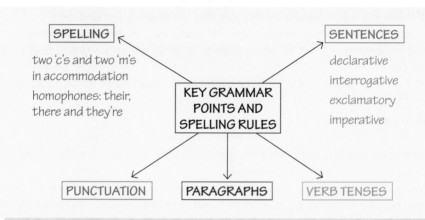

Quick quiz

Answer these quick questions about grammar, punctuation and spelling.

1. What is a simple sentence?
2. What is a compound sentence?
3. What is a complex sentence?
4. Explain what a declarative sentence is.
5. When would you use an interrogative sentence?
6. Explain what an exclamatory sentence is.
7. Explain what an imperative sentence is.
8. What tense would you mainly use when writing to give your viewpoint?
9. When would you use a comma in a sentence?
10. Why would you use a semicolon in a sentence?
11. Why would you use round brackets in a sentence?
12. When would you use reported speech?
13. When do you need to start a new paragraph?
14. Name four connectives that you could use in your viewpoint writing.
15. Explain the difference between the homophones 'their', 'there' and 'they're'.

Practise your skills

Read this short extract from an article, then answer the practice task.

> Swiming is an essential skill that all children need in there lives. Why is swimming important you ask Imagine the number of times that you have used this skill swimming can quite literally save your life! It was also great exarcise a fun way to keep fit and active.

Q: Copy the extract, correcting the mistakes. Look out for:
- places where punctuation is missing
- spelling errors
- verbs in the incorrect tense.

Power paragraphs

Read this paragraph from a speech, then answer the practice task.

> Have you ever wondered why jewellery is such an important issue in schools. Jewellery has long been a way to express yourself. A necklace or earrings can show that you are indivdiual and make you feel special. Why do schools insist on controlling students so that they can't even choose what earrings they wear? Jewellery can also have personal significance. A gift from a loved one can bring comfort and why should students be prevented from that comfort just because they are in school.

Q: Proofread the paragraph. Rewrite it, making corrections and paying particular attention to:
- use of punctuation
- paragraphing
- use of connectives
- the range of sentence types.

VIEWPOINT WRITING
Non-fiction text types

What will you have to do?

- The **writing task** in **Question 5** will ask you to focus on **expressing a viewpoint**.
- There are several different types of **non-fiction** text that you could be asked to write. **Each text type** has **different structure or layout** conventions.
- Remember – the layout and organisation are important but a **large number of the marks** will be awarded for the way you **develop the content** of your text.
- See 'Persuasive language techniques' on pages 52–53 for further details on **how to add evidence to your argument**.

What texts could you be asked to write?

The key text types you could be asked to write are outlined below.

Text type	What is this?
Letter	This is likely to be a formal letter with a formal audience, e.g. a headteacher or town council.
Article	This will usually be for a newspaper or magazine. If the audience for this is adults, it should be formal in style.
Leaflet	An informative sheet, usually divided into sections. Leaflets come through our letterboxes, are inserted into newspapers, left in shops or handed out in the street. You will usually be asked to write a leaflet that gives information and persuades your audience on a particular topic, e.g. to change the voting age to 16.
Speech	A spoken presentation but written down. You will need to imagine yourself delivering this speech to a specified audience, like a politician might on a TV broadcast. It is important that the speech is clear and well organised for your audience.
Essay	An essay is similar to a speech but it is written to be read rather than listened to. It might be published in a journal or newspaper.

HOW do I write a letter?

Key features of a letter
- Address at the top of the letter (in the exam, it can be imaginary)
- Date
- Correct form of address (Dear Sir/Madam/the name of the recipient)
- Correct form of signing off (Yours sincerely/faithfully)
- Clear introduction outlining your argument
- Clear conclusion, which calls for action, e.g. *'Please support me to ensure that students are not required to wear uniform to school.'*

How can you approach it?
- It is likely that you will be asked to write a formal letter so it is important to use the key features of a formal letter, as outlined above.
- The main body of your letter will use similar techniques to an essay or a speech with a key set of ideas to get across.

HOW do I write an article or a leaflet?

Key features of an article
- Clear title or headline (try to be creative and original)
- A strapline (a catchy subheading beneath the title)
- Subheadings
- Brief introduction
- Well-organised/sequenced paragraphs
- A personal voice or opinion

Key features of a leaflet
- Clear title (try to be creative and original) and strapline
- Organisational elements, e.g. sub-sections with subheadings/boxes/bullet points
- Well-organised/sequenced paragraphs
- You may use imperatives to encourage the reader to do something

How can you approach them?
- Key features for organising an article or a leaflet are a title, strapline and subheadings.
- Decide on your viewpoint before you begin writing. Will you need to use the first or third person? What will be the tone of your text?
- Make sure that when you plan your ideas, you organise them well so that your subheadings make your writing clearer.
- Choose the words for your title carefully. Try to use repetition or a play on words in the title to grab the reader's attention.

Note it!

Remember to organise your letter clearly using paragraphs. Use a new paragraph to indicate that you are moving on to the next point.

How do I write a speech or an essay?

These text types are very similar in the way that they are organised.

Key features of a speech
- Clear introduction that addresses the audience
- Direct address to the audience throughout (use questions, second person, etc.)
- Well-organised/sequenced paragraphs
- Clear ending that addresses the audience

Key features of an essay
- Effective introduction that introduces your key ideas
- Well-organised/sequenced paragraphs
- Clearly focused conclusion

How can you approach them?
- A key feature of the organisation of these text types is sequencing your ideas so that they flow clearly through the paragraphs.
- When you write your plan, number your points so that you have a planned sequence. It is usually a good idea to begin with your most powerful and convincing points.

Putting it into practice

Read the statement below.

'Mobile phones are damaging education as they provide a constant distraction and mean that students do not work as hard as they should. Phones should therefore be banned from schools with immediate effect.'

Now think about what differences there might be in text type if you were asked to respond to this statement.

The task might ask you to:

1. Write a letter to your headteacher arguing your point of view on this statement.
2. Write an article for a local newspaper in which you explain your point of view on this statement.
3. Write the text of a speech that you would give to the school council in which you argue for or against this statement.

Note it!

Your ideas may well be the same for each of these tasks. It is the way that you organise and shape them that changes with each text type.

How can I write an effective opening?

Read these two openings of non-fiction responses to tasks 1 and 2.

1

25 School Road
Hightown
Bedfordshire

21 May 2019

Dear Mr Masters,
I am writing with great concern regarding the recent debate surrounding the role of phones in schools. Why has the internet come to symbolise something bad when it promotes so much good? Using phones to access online content is a powerful force for educating all; across all walks of society people can learn, grow and develop by accessing information that is often available free of charge.

2

WHERE IS THE 'SMART' IN SMARTPHONES?
Why phones should not be seen as the future of our education
There is no denying the power of phones. At the touch of a screen, across all levels of society, people can learn, grow and develop by accessing information in an instant. Do phones have a role to play in education? Most would argue 'yes'. Do they belong in schools? The answer to this may be very different.

Now you try!

Now write the opening to a speech to your school council, responding to the same statement.

'Mobile phones are damaging education as they provide a constant distraction and mean that students do not work as hard as they should do. Phones should therefore be banned from schools with immediate effect.'

Decide whether you will argue for or against.

Remember to:

- plan carefully, including an introduction and a conclusion
- use a range of persuasive techniques
- use a convincing voice

What will you have to do?

- You will be given **one writing task** that will ask you to **express a viewpoint**.
- You will be presented with **a debatable statement.** This will help you **develop ideas to support your opinion**. The task follows this statement and will indicate the purpose, form and audience for your writing, like this:

> **5.** 'The pursuit of extreme sports is too dangerous. The media must not promote these activities as they encourage children to take unnecessary risks.'
>
> Write a letter to a student newspaper in which you explain your point of view on this statement.

Why is reading the task important?

You need to read the task to find the purpose, audience and form of the writing.

- **Purpose**: what the writing is intended to do, e.g. persuade others to change their opinion.
- **Audience**: who it is aimed at, e.g. the age group, interests, etc.
- **Form**: the type of writing required, e.g. a letter, an article, the text for a speech.

How will this help me to plan?

Once you have identified the purpose, audience and form, this will help you plan and craft your piece of writing effectively.

You could also add the register and tone to develop your plan further.

Register: the type of language used in a text, especially how formal it is.

Tone: the writer's apparent attitude towards the subject, e.g. humorous, angry, critical or passionate.

Putting it into practice

> **5.** 'The pursuit of extreme sports is too dangerous. The media must not promote these activities as they encourage children to take unnecessary risks.'
>
> Write a letter to a student newspaper in which you explain your point of view on this statement.

Tone = enthusiastic and committed, but clear for age group; could add humour
Form
Audience
Register = formal
Purpose

How can I write with a clear viewpoint?

Read this extract from a successful response.

Extreme sports are increasingly popular. Many adults have engaged in such activities and regard them as some of the most rewarding experiences of their lives. So why are children judged so harshly for wanting to do the same thing? We are surely capable of understanding the dangers. When interviewed, Luke, an 18-year-old student, said 'climbing to Everest Base Camp was the best experience of my life'. Extreme sports can give children the confidence and determination to succeed in all areas of life.

Uses clear and formal register; newspaper article form signalled by clear opening statement

Persuasive purpose shown by rhetorical question; maintains passionate and committed tone

First-person plural used to include the audience

Use of direct speech to give a personal perspective to connect with the audience (students)

Note it!

Use a fairly formal register in your response, even for a student audience. Your tone may shift (e.g. from humorous to serious) but should not change in formality dramatically.

Now you try!

Identify the register and tone that you would use for the task below.

Then write the opening paragraph of your response.

5. 'Reality TV brings out the worst qualities in people and should be banned from all TV channels. It models low standards of behaviour and contributes nothing to our society.'

Write an article for a magazine in which you argue for or against this statement.

My progress   Needs more work ☐   Getting there ☐   Sorted! ☐   51

HOW can persuasive language help express a viewpoint?

Rhetorical devices

- Rhetorical devices are persuasive language techniques that have **powerful effects** on the reader.
- They can help you **connect emotionally with your audience**, asking them to empathise, understand and agree with your viewpoint.

What rhetorical devices could you use?

Device	Explanation	Examples
Tricolon (triple, triad)	Using three words or phrases in a row, often with the most powerful word coming last	*Free information via the internet promotes education, growth and independence.*
Rhetorical question	A question that makes a point rather than seeking an answer	*Why has the internet come to symbolise something bad, when it promotes so much good?*
Alliteration	Repeated use of consonant sounds at the start of words; often used with other rhetorical devices	*Let us all learn to live with one another peacefully, rather than come into conflict.*
Parallelism	Achieving contrast by repeating a grammatical form	*Let us all learn to live with others peacefully, rather than clash with others violently.*

What evidence should you use?

As well as rhetorical devices, you should use evidence to support your viewpoint. This will add weight to your argument to persuade your audience. Evidence could include:

- An **anecdote** – a very short story, e.g. *'Running around the school athletic track yesterday, my fitness app on my phone told me that my heart rate was lower than on last week's run.'*
- Referring to '**experts**' – this could refer to a study or to other more informal 'research', e.g. *'A study published in 2018 found that ...'* or *'Many students I have spoken to say that ...'.*

- **Statistics** – using numbers to support your argument, e.g. *'87% of students say that they rely on online material to complete their studies.'*
- You could also refer to the **sources** in Section A of the exam paper, if you think they are relevant.

Putting it into practice

- The best way to ensure that you use rhetorical devices in the exam is to add them to your plan before you begin writing. This will make sure that you connect your ideas to your use of language.

- Look at how this is done for the first point, in response to the following question, in the essay plan below.

> **5.** 'School uniform is an out-of-date tradition. It is used to control students and prevents freedom of expression.'
>
> Write an essay for a competition in which you argue for or against this statement.

Rhetorical question: Why do we still need it? ⟶ No – out of date – not fit for modern times ⟵ Tricolon: focus on uniform being obsolete

School uniform – Is it still valuable?

Note it!

Try not to use too many rhetorical devices in one paragraph. Spread them throughout your writing.

Exam focus

How can I write persuasively?

Read this opening from a successful response.

School uniform – outdated, old fashioned and obsolete. Why do we still need it in these modern times? It seems to me that it is time for schools to wake up and join us in the twenty-first century, and fast.

	Tricolon
	Rhetorical question
	Alliteration

Now you try!

Write another paragraph for the speech above. Explore the point that school uniform can be uncomfortable to wear. Try to use two rhetorical devices and add an anecdote to support your argument.

VIEWPOINT WRITING
Persuading effectively

HOW can persuasive language strengthen an argument?

- An **effective argument connects closely with its reader**. **Literary techniques** and emotive language can be used to do this in your writing.
- The most commonly used literary techniques are similes, metaphors and personification.
- **Emotive language** can also be used to **provoke an emotional response** in the reader.

Putting it into practice

Look at how the examples in the table use these techniques. Then consider their intended effects.

Technique	Examples	Intended effect
Simile	*Attitudes towards school uniform are as out of date as horse-drawn carriages. They are stuck in the past and are not fit for purpose.*	Attitudes towards school uniform are compared to horse-drawn carriages to emphasise how out of date they are. They do not belong in modern society.
Metaphor	*We should free our children from the shackles of school uniform.*	School uniform is compared to shackles (chains) to stress how the writer sees it as controlling children.
Personification	*It is time for schools to wake up and join us in the twenty-first century.*	Schools are personified to illustrate how they are out of date: they are 'asleep' and should 'wake up' and react.
Emotive language	*It is time to end the unnecessary suffering of students and give us a chance to express ourselves.*	The focus on suffering invites the reader to consider things from students' perspectives. The plea 'give us a chance' reinforces how unfair the situation is.

Choose two of the literary techniques from the table and write your own examples, based on the idea of school uniform being outdated.

Exam focus

How can I use literary techniques? A05

Read the passage below and evaluate how these techniques have been used. The student is writing about the importance of a tax on sugary foods.

> Sugary foods and drinks have become the nemesis of our generation – they lie in wait – ready to wreak havoc in years to come on the health of our nation. Is it already too late for us to take action? The problem is that the possible consequences of a high intake of sugar are not immediately obvious. It could take 20 or 30 years for this monster to rear its ugly head in the shape of diabetes, heart disease or worse.

Emotive language

Personification

Metaphor

Now you try!

Now read this passage, which could follow the one above. Is it as convincing as the paragraph above? Redraft it to add at least two literary devices.

Note it!

Focus on trying to create a convincing image. Your language technique will only work if your reader understands and believes it. Don't overuse the techniques!

> A tax on sugar is the best way forward if we want to solve this problem. Although there is a problem, I know that we can solve it with a tax. Sugary drinks are bad for us, so we have to do something about this. We can do this by using a tax, educating children and changing the way that school dinners work.

How can you use structure to organise your ideas effectively?

- Structuring your ideas clearly is one way to make your argument effective.
- Clear organisation is important within each paragraph and in the way you link paragraphs together throughout your whole response.

Structure across the whole text

An effective text usually contains:

- a clear and convincing opening paragraph that identifies key idea/s
- points organised in a logical sequence (beginning with the most powerful)
- clear paragraphs, with a new paragraph for each new point
- links between paragraphs to show how points develop the overall argument (using **topic sentences** and **connectives**) – for more, see pages 40–41
- a clear conclusion (see 'Planning and structuring a response' on pages 62–64).

Structure within paragraphs

Effective paragraphs usually:

- focus on exploring one central idea
- begin with a topic sentence
- develop the idea further (using evidence, for example)
- use connectives to link points.

Putting it into practice

Plan for one paragraph in response to the task below.

5. 'The views of young people are ignored in our society. The voting age should be lowered to 16 so that young people have an opportunity to express their views on political issues.'

Write a letter to your local MP explaining your viewpoint on this statement.

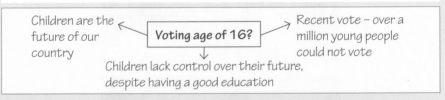

What connectives could you add to the plan to link these ideas within the paragraph?

Exam focus

How can I write a structured paragraph?

Read this example of an effective paragraph using the plan on page 56. Note that the student has also used the persuasive techniques explored on pages 52–53.

What is more important to a society than its young people? Children work hard to get an education to prepare for their future, but is their future really theirs? In a recent political vote, it was suggested that the opinions of over a million young people were not considered as they were below the age of 18. Consequently, these young people will have to suffer in silence because their voices are not heard. It is time for change; we all need to work together to transform society for the better.

Clear topic sentence	
Another rhetorical question	
Inclusion of statistics develops the idea	
Connective to link sentences	
Summarises the point; a call to action	

Note it!

Remember that Question 5 is about viewpoints – you need to have a consistent opinion. Don't change your mind half way through writing your response.

Now you try!

Write at least one paragraph in response to the task below.

5. 'Veganism is an important way to help save the planet, as it lessens the impact that humans have. Schools should encourage students to become vegan and offer vegan choices on their menus.'

   Write a letter to your headteacher and school governors explaining your viewpoint on this statement.

Look at the mind-map representing elements of viewpoint writing. Is there anything else you could add?

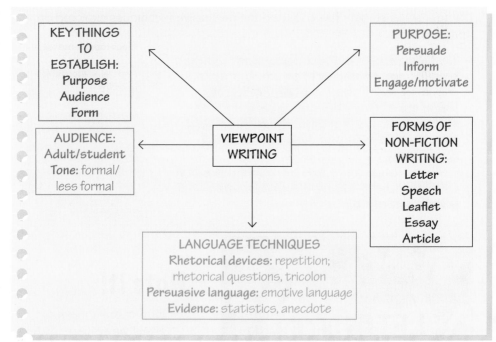

Quick quiz

Answer these quick questions about different aspects of viewpoint writing.

1. What text type should end with 'Yours sincerely' or 'Yours faithfully'?

2. Which two text types need a title at the beginning of the text?

3. For which text type should you use subheadings, boxes and other organisational features?

4. What is the second person and how could you use it in your text?

5. Explain what the key terms 'purpose', 'audience' and 'form' mean.

6. Explain the key term 'register'.

7. Explain the key term 'tone'.

8. Name at least two rhetorical devices you could use in your writing.

9. What is a tricolon?

10. What three types of evidence could you use in your text to develop your ideas?

11. What is the difference between a simile and a metaphor?

12. When should you use a topic sentence?

13. Name at least three connectives that you could use in your writing.

14. How many ideas should you explore in each paragraph?

15. When should you start a new paragraph?

Practise your skills

Read this opening section from a piece of viewpoint/persuasive writing.

> I do think that schools waste too much paper. Teachers are constantly giving out handouts, which students then lose. Why can't these be shared online? Students could work on phones or tablets, which would mean that we would no longer need to use paper in school.

Q: How could it be improved? Look out for:
- places where connectives could be added
- places where you could add a rhetorical device or persuasive language
- ideas where more evidence is needed.

Power paragraphs

1. Write out your finished paragraph/s from the task above.

2. Then read the beginning of an article below, which argues that too much food is wasted while some people go hungry.

> WASTE NOT, WANT NOT
>
> Food is something that most of us take for granted. What would you say if you discovered that 89 million tonnes of food is wasted every year? And that is just in the European Union.

Continue the article, writing up to 100 words more in a new paragraph of your own. Remember to use rhetorical devices and to add evidence with statistics, anecdotes or expert opinions.

Five key things about Paper 2, Section B

1. Paper 2, Section B contains **a single question (Question 5)** on an issue related to the topic of the sources in Section A. The question usually requires you to express your own viewpoint on a given statement.

2. You will be told both what **form** to write in, e.g. a letter, a speech or a magazine article, and the **audience** for the task.

3. Remember: the focus is **writers' viewpoints and perspectives**. Use the writer's skills that you identified and analysed in Section A: Reading if you can.

4. Spend about **45 minutes** on the whole task. First spend **5–10 minutes planning your response**. Then take **35 minutes** to **write your response**.

5. Allow **5 minutes** to **check your writing** at the end. Look out especially for mistakes in **spelling**, **punctuation** and **grammar**.

What skills will the writing question test?

The table below gives an overview of the skills and content expected in your response to the writing task. It also shows how the marks are allocated.

Marks	What you must do
24	**Content and organisation (AO5)** • Adopt an **appropriate writing style** (e.g. writing persuasively). • Choose **interesting ideas** that are raised by the question. • Use a **range of evidence** to support your argument. • Organise your writing for **clarity** and **interest**, using paragraphs with **connectives** and **discourse markers** (e.g. 'However') to link them where necessary. • Ensure your writing is convincing and persuasive, e.g. connecting with the reader by using a range of persuasive language features.
16	**Technical accuracy (AO6)** • Check that you have used **paragraphing** correctly to organise and develop your argument. • Check **grammar**, especially **sentence types;** use a range of **different sentence types** to support your argument. • Check your **spelling** and **punctuation**.

What do I need to do to get a good mark?

Use this grid to understand what your current level is and how to improve it.

	AO5 Content and organisation	**AO6 Technical accuracy**
High	**Content** • You use a **convincing** register matched to audience and purpose • You have an **extensive and ambitious vocabulary** • You sustain writing with **well-crafted linguistic devices** **Organisation** • You use **varied and inventive** structural features • You use **fluently linked paragraphs** with **integrated** connectives	• You have **consistently secure, accurate sentences** and use the **full range** of sentence forms • You use a **wide range of punctuation**, with high accuracy • You use Standard English **consistently** with **secure control of complex grammar** • You have an **extensive, ambitious vocabulary** • Your **spelling** is **highly accurate**
Mid	**Content** • Your register is **consistently matched** to **audience and purpose** • You have an **increasingly sophisticated** vocabulary • You use a **range of successful linguistic devices** **Organisation** • You use **effective structural features** • You use **paragraphs in a clear way** with **integrated** connectives	• You have **mostly secure, accurate sentences** and use a **variety** of sentence forms. • You have a **range of punctuation**, mostly accurate • Your use of **Standard English** is **mostly consistent** • You have an **increasingly sophisticated** vocabulary • Your **spelling** is **generally accurate**
Lower	**Content** • You **attempt** to match **register** to **audience** and **purpose** • You make **conscious use** of **vocabulary** • You use **some linguistic devices** **Organisation** • You make **some use** of **structural features** • You make **some use of paragraphs** and **ways of connecting them**, if not always successfully	• You sometimes use a **variety** of sentence forms • You have **some control** of **punctuation** • Your use of **Standard English** varies with **some control** • You use a **simple vocabulary** • Your **basic spelling** is **usually accurate**, but you make mistakes with more ambitious words

Read this sample exam-style writing task

5. 'Many students do not enjoy compulsory sport in schools. As a result, many end up hating physical activity, which has a negative impact on their later lives. Compulsory sport should therefore be removed from the curriculum.'

Write a speech that you will deliver to your teachers arguing for or against this statement.

(24 marks for content and organisation; 16 marks for technical accuracy)

[40 marks]

How do you plan your viewpoint response?

- **Read the question. Highlight key words** and then **annotate them**.
- Quickly **generate ideas** for your response. Remember to **include evidence** to support them.
- **Plan the order** of your paragraphs. Remember to **note connectives**.
- Think about and **plan** (if time allows) **your opening and closing paragraphs**.

Note it!

It is definitely worth planning your response, but if you find that you have better ideas while writing, do not feel you have to stick to your plan.

What do I focus on?

- Highlight the key words.
- Identify the form, audience and purpose. Think about how these will influence your writing.
- Think about the register and tone. What would work best for the set task?

5. 'Many students do not enjoy compulsory sport in schools. As a result, many end up hating physical activity, which has a negative impact on their later lives. Compulsory sport should therefore be removed from the curriculum.'

Write a speech that you will deliver to your teachers arguing for or against this statement.

Form; register = formal	
Audience	
Purpose	
Tone = passionate and committed	

How do I get my ideas?

Once you have identified the key words, use a table to quickly note down your initial ideas. For example:

Compulsory sport should be removed	Compulsory sport should remain
• Students have only limited choices of sports; can't choose to suit their strengths • Too much focus on team sports • Can be humiliating – creates unnecessary stress and worry for students who are not good at sport • Makes students afraid of taking part in sport as adults	• Fun • Good for wellbeing/mental health • Brings a range of skills: team work – good for future employment • Good habits for later life – staying fit and healthy • Health crisis – some primary school children are very unfit

How do I organise my ideas?

Plan carefully. From reading the question, planning should take you 5-10 minutes or even up to 15, but experts say that the better the plan, the better the outcome.

- Select three or four key arguments.
- Sequence your ideas so that you have a clear order to your argument.
- Include evidence for your ideas in your plan – use statistics/experts/**anecdotes** to add detail to your ideas.
- Add connectives to your plan to link your ideas together.
- Think about your use of persuasive language techniques and devices. How will you use language to persuade?

See the sample plan on page 64.

Note it!

The statistics, experts and anecdotes you use to give evidence can be real or made up.

Read through this sample plan for the viewpoint writing task on page 62.

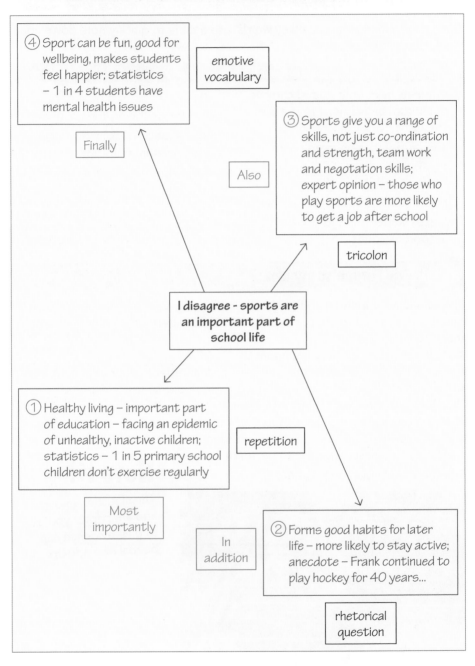

④ Sport can be fun, good for wellbeing, makes students feel happier; statistics – 1 in 4 students have mental health issues

emotive vocabulary

Finally

③ Sports give you a range of skills, not just co-ordination and strength, team work and negotation skills; expert opinion – those who play sports are more likely to get a job after school

Also

tricolon

I disagree - sports are an important part of school life

① Healthy living – important part of education – facing an epidemic of unhealthy, inactive children; statistics – 1 in 5 primary school children don't exercise regularly

repetition

Most importantly

In addition

② Forms good habits for later life – more likely to stay active; anecdote – Frank continued to play hockey for 40 years...

rhetorical question

How can I craft effective opening and closing paragraphs?

The opening and closing paragraphs of this task are very important. They show the examiner that you understand how to organise the whole text.

Opening

- Use your opening paragraph to grab the reader's attention.
- As this is a speech, use direct address and a rhetorical question to involve the reader.

Sport is something that we can all enjoy. It helps with our health, wellbeing and social interaction. There are games options to suit everyone, whether you prefer team or individual sports. If you take this opportunity away from students, it will only have a negative impact on their lives. Why would you remove sport from the curriculum when it has so many benefits for all?

Short sentence clearly shows viewpoint; use of inclusive first-person plural 'we'.

Tricolon shows the range of benefits of sport.

Conditional clause suggests the negative impact of taking away sports.

Rhetorical question addresses the reader, engaging them with this viewpoint.

Closing (conclusion)

- Make sure you link your closing paragraph to your opening one. This shows that you have clearly responded to the statement.
- Remember to try and finish with a clear sense of what your argument is.

As I am sure you will agree, sport is such a fundamental part of school life that the mere thought of removing it would make us all very worried. Our physical and mental state, as well as our social wellbeing, is of central importance, both to us personally and to the whole school community. For these reasons, I am sure you will support my plea to retain compulsory sport on the school curriculum.

Direct address encourages empathy and agreement with the writer's viewpoint.

Subordinate clause reinforces the importance of sport.

Balanced argument is reflected in the balance of sentence construction and 'both'.

Cause emphasises strong statement of viewpoint at the end.

Note it!

Remember to check your points against your plan as you are writing.

What does a Grade 5 response look like?

Read the viewpoint writing task again, then the **Grade 5** response below.

5. 'Many students do not enjoy compulsory sport in schools. As a result, many end up hating physical activity, which has a negative impact on their later lives. Compulsory sport should therefore be removed from the curriculum.'

   Write a speech that you will deliver to your teachers arguing for or against this statement.

   (24 marks for content and organisation; 16 marks for technical accuracy)

   [40 marks]

Sport is something that I have always enjoyed. It helps students to stay healthy, so it is really important that they keep sports in school so that all children can benefit from joining in.
Healthy living is very important. Schools should be making sure that they promote healthy living as it is an important part of every child's education. We are facing a massive problem with unhealthy children spending too much time on their phones or gaming.
A statistic suggests that one in five primary age children don't exercise regularly. This is a shocking figure that makes us realise that it is time to start taking healthy living seriously.
Does it really make a difference to play sport at school? If you play sports at school, you will continue and therefore have a healthier life. In a recent interview, Frank said he is still playing hockey for the local club at the age of 80. He is still fit and healthy, and this is all down to playing sports at school. We should all aim to be like Frank and, if we play sports at school, we have more chance of carrying on with sports in later life like Frank does.
Sport can also give you a range of other skills. It can keep you fit and strong, but can also teach you to work as a team and how to work with others.

AO5 Communication generally clear

AO5 Attempts to use correct style and register

AO5 Uses statistic as evidence

AO5 Persuasive use of rhetorical question

AO6 Variety of relevant ideas well linked in a complex sentence

AO6 Attempts a variety of sentence forms

These skills are vital for life beyond school as many students don't have much opportunity to develop them outside of school. An expert said that students who play team sports are more likely to get a good job once they leave school. Sports can therefore make your life better! Sport can also be fun! Statistics have suggested that stress is a real problem these days, with one in four students suffering with mental health issues. Sport can help with this, distracting teenagers from their screens and encouraging them to get out of the house and feel better. Sport has the power to change lives and make lives better for everyone.

We interviewed a range of teenagers as to their views and 80% of them said that they would join in with sport more often if it was fun. Dodgeball, swimming and zumba were all suggested as examples of this. By listening to students, we have a chance to make change for the better.

I hope you will agree, now that you have heard my argument, that sport is such an important part of school life that we cannot remove it from the timetable. Our students' future health and happiness rests on this. So please keep sport on the curriculum – for good.

AO6 Vocabulary clearly chosen for effect

AO6 Attempts to include an expert view

AO6 Uses a range of vocabulary

AO5 Interview and statistics used as evidence to give credibility to the argument

AO6 Uses of a range of punctuation

Check the skills

Reread the opening paragraph of the response. Improve this section by:
- Introducing two persuasive language devices
- Using a wider range of sentence types
- Using a wider range of vocabulary for effect.

Now you try!

Write a full plan in response to this task.

5. 'The views of young people are ignored in our society. The voting age should be moved to 16 so that young people have an opportunity to express their views on political issues.'

Write a letter to your local MP explaining your viewpoint on this statement.

What does a Grade 7+ response look like?

Now read the **Grade 7+** response below to the school sport task.

Sport is something that we can all enjoy. It helps with our health, wellbeing and social interaction. If you take this opportunity away from students it will only have a negative impact on their lives. Why would you remove sport from the curriculum when it has so many benefits for all?

> **AO5** Communication consistently clear

> **AO5** Persuasive use of rhetorical question

Learning how to live a healthy life is such an important part of every child's education; why would we jeopardise it by taking away the opportunity for children to participate in sports at school? We are facing a health crisis; many people no longer know what healthy living is because they are too focused on the digital world. The government suggests that one in five primary age children do not exercise regularly, which is putting lives at risk. It is time to put healthy living back on the agenda.

> **AO6** Effective use of variety of sentence forms

Yet, does it really make a difference? I would argue that involving students in sports is about ensuring that they stay active in later life – healthy habits stick. I recently interviewed Frank who, at the age of 80, is still playing hockey for his local club. He claims that his active lifestyle has kept him fit and healthy; while his friends are having hip replacements, he is out playing hockey and walking the dog. An active lifestyle should be an aspiration for us all, young or old, and sport at school is the firm foundation that students need to begin this lifelong journey.

> **AO5** Well-embedded use of anecdote

> **AO5** Clear and consistent style and register

In addition to the health benefits, sports give you a range of skills that are essential in life. As well as fitness, co-ordination and strength, sports also encourage students to learn to work as a team and to interact with others face to face, skills that students are in dire need of in a world that is increasingly virtual. An expert from the University of London suggested that students who play team

> **AO5** Range of clear, connected ideas

> **AO6** Sophisticated vocabulary chosen for effect

> **AO5** Includes expert view effectively

sports are more likely to be successful in jobs once they leave full-time education. Sports can therefore literally change lives for the better, creating students who are fitter, healthier and wealthier.

Most importantly, sport can be fun! Worrying statistics stress how difficult lives are for students these days with one in four students suffering from some form of mental health issue. Sport can improve lives, taking students away from their screens and improving their wellbeing through fresh air, exercise and interaction with others. If we want to reverse this worrying trend, we need to act now.

Ultimately, sport has the power to change us for the better. Interviews conducted with students revealed that over 80% would participate in sports if the options available were seen as more 'fun'. It is time for our voice to be heard – even if it is us singing slightly out of tune as we dance, enjoying ourselves in our weekly zumba class.

As I am sure you will agree, sport is such a fundamental part of school life that the mere thought of removing it makes us all very worried. Our physical and mental state as well as our social wellbeing is of central importance, both to us personally and the whole school community. I am sure you will support my plea to retain compulsory sport on the school curriculum.

AO6 Example of range of punctuation used, mostly with success

AO5 Strong use of statistic as evidence

AO5 Embeds reference to research/statistics within the argument

AO5 Effective use of humour to engage the audience

AO6 Increasingly sophisticated vocabulary reinforces closing points

Check the skills

Identify the ways in which the Grade 7+ response is better than the Grade 5 response on pages 66–67. Using the annotations to help you, make notes on:
- Clarity of the ideas and argument
- Use of persuasive language devices
- Appropriate register and style
- Choice and range of vocabulary
- Variety of sentence forms.

Now you try!

Now, using your plan from page 67, write a full response to the persuasive writing task about lowering the voting age to 16.

Source A: Twentieth-century non-fiction

This extract is from a newspaper article written by Jenna Thompson that was published in The Guardian *in December 2017.*

> *Over the festive period, Abbeyfield homes will provide activities, meals and accommodation for hundreds of visitors*

Each Christmas, my staff and I put on a performance for our residents, their families and older people from the community near our home in West Sussex. This year, we had songs, poems and readings about the different chapters of people's lives – from being a toddler, to growing up, falling in love and getting
5   married, through to older years.

Midway through a performance, while a screen displayed a slideshow of photos of our residents and their families from the last year, I caught a glimpse of 93-year-old Pat in the front row, singing along.

Before moving in to our home, Pat had become increasingly isolated, despite
10   living with her family. She was adamant she wasn't going to move into a care home, and when she did come to live with us, she made it clear that she would keep herself to herself. Gradually though, she started to get involved in activities at the house and we encouraged her to talk to us and other residents.

Abbeyfield was founded more than 60 years ago by Richard Carr-Gomm,
15   a former Coldstream guard, with the aim of easing the crippling loneliness experienced by a forgotten generation of older people. For Carr-Gomm, companionship was just as important as putting a roof over someone's head.

Research shows that nearly a million older people feel lonelier at Christmas time. The festive period can be particularly distressing for them, as it can
20   amplify feelings of loss, bereavement and isolation.

Abbeyfield's Companionship at Christmas campaign aims to combat this by opening up our homes to older people who live alone. For the past eight years, more than 500 Abbeyfield houses across the country have provided activities, meals and overnight stays so that people don't have to wake up to an empty
25   house on Christmas Day. Around 600 older people enjoy the warmth and companionship of Abbeyfield at our events.

Our houses act as community hubs – and throughout the year, house managers and their teams work hard to build links with community groups and partners such as Age UK, local church groups and smaller charities to let people know
30   what we do. We also rely on the media to help us spread the word about the campaign, so we can reach and engage with those older people who are hardest to reach.

For 76-year-old Alma, who lives alone following her husband's death three years ago, Christmas is a difficult time because the clubs and groups she keeps
35 herself busy with stop over the festive period.

"You don't want to be pushing yourself on to someone else's family on Christmas Day, even though people do ask," she says. "I don't have any children myself. My sister and her family live a long way from me – and like so many people these days, they're very busy with their own lives and assume I am busy
40 with mine, so I would just spend Christmas alone."

Last year, things changed after Alma read about the Companionship at Christmas campaign.

"When I first read about it at my local library I couldn't believe it could be true," she says. "It is a wonderful thing. I no longer felt I was imposing on
45 someone else – and I could look forward to a Christmas with company and people around me."

https://www.theguardian.com/social-care-network/2017/dec/19/care-homes-
christmas-lonely-older-people

Source B: Nineteenth-century non-fiction

This extract is from an article written by Charles Dickens in 1850, taken from the weekly magazine Household Words.

Christmas among the London Poor and Sick

Out of the family parties, two millions and a quarter strong, assembled in London, some eight or a hundred thousand have their Christmas dinner provided for them by their respective parishes. Their **pauper**-hood does not sink them below the reach of the **genial** season. Christmas finds them out, even in their wards and their
5 day-rooms. A cheerful bustle betokens the welcome day. An extra polish is seen on workhouse shoes; here and there, a stray morsel of finery, or a special evidence of neatness, is visible in workhouse garments. The workhouse chapel has a spray or two of the green emblems of the season, and the sermon has an extra spice of geniality. The dining-room has quite an exhilarating polish. The white bare walls
10 are warmed up with their sprigs of holly, and the tables – well scrubbed as usual – are graced by the promised feast. No *skilly* to-day – but beef! No hard dumplings, but plum pudding! The plums are not stoned, and there's no brandy sauce; but the appetites are not **epicurean**.

But, the huge **prandial** army of eighty to a hundred thousand paupers in London
15 do not all feast in the workhouses. In round numbers, only about twenty thousand, young and old, are so accommodated. The majority are out-door poor, who enjoy anything they may receive at their own lodgings. The number of both classes had greatly diminished last year as compared with the previous twelve months. It is anticipated that Christmas, 1850, will show a still greater reduction in the number
20 of persons dependent on charity for their holiday meal.

Of the twenty thousand who usually partake of workhouse beef and plum-pudding in the metropolis, the largest party assemble in Marylebone. In the workhouse of that parish, last year, nearly two thousand paupers were feasted. The City of London, in its establishment at Bow, and at the Norwood Schools, fed the next
25 largest number: their ranks mustering altogether some sixteen hundred. Third in the list, stood St. Pancras, who fed on Christmas Day, of young and old, sick and well, more than thirteen hundred. To the East of this Modern Babylon for the two next great Christmas gatherings, and we find them in Stepney and Whitechapel – each gathering, together, upwards of a thousand candidates for beef and pudding.
30 Across the river, we have the next strong parties; in Lambeth, and the two Southwark parishes; after these, follow a list of places where snug sets of seven hundred, six hundred, five hundred, assembled. Unfashionable St. George in the East musters only two hundred more than aristocratic St. James, whilst such suburban places as Edmonton and Kensington display the fewest candidates for
35 parish fare.

From *Household Words* by Charles Dickens, 21 December 1850

Glossary

pauper a poor person

genial friendly and cheerful

skilly a thin broth made with oatmeal and water and flavoured with meat

epicurean a person devoted to the enjoyment of fine food and drink

prandial during or related to dinner/lunch

Section A: Reading

Answer **all** questions in this section.

You are advised to spend about 45 minutes on this section.

1. Reread the first section of **Source A** from **lines 1 to 13**.

   Choose **four** statements below which are TRUE.

   A Each Christmas the staff at Abbeyfield put on a performance just for the residents.

   B The performance is about the different times in people's lives.

   C They perform songs, poems and readings.

   D The screenshow showed pictures of the residents' previous lives.

   E 93-year-old Pat was enjoying the performance.

   F Pat moved to the care home because she lived alone.

   G Pat did not want to move to the care home.

   H Pat did not join in once she moved to the care home.

   [4 marks]

2. You need to refer to **Source A** and **Source B** for this question.

Both extracts describe the arrangements made for Christmas.

Use the details from **both** sources. Write a summary of the similarities of the arrangements made to celebrate Christmas. **[8 marks]**

3. You now need to refer **only** to Source B, **lines 1–13**.

How does the writer use language to describe the positive atmosphere at the Christmas celebrations? **[12 marks]**

4. For this question, you need to refer to the **whole of Source A**, together with the **whole of Source B**.

Compare how the two writers convey their similar perspectives on people's enjoyment of Christmas.

In your answer, you could:

● compare their similar perspectives

● compare the methods the writers use to convey their similar perspectives

● support your response with references to both texts. **[16 marks]**

Section B: Writing

You are advised to spend about 45 minutes on this section.

Write in full sentences.

You are reminded of the need to plan your answer.

You should leave enough time to check your work at the end.

5. 'Religious festivals should be a time of kindness, not a competition to see who can get the most expensive gift. Advertising at times of such festivals should be banned to stop the mindless spending of money and to encourage people to focus on the real meaning of that time of year.'

Write an article for a newspaper in which you explain your point of view on this statement.

(24 marks for content and organisation

16 marks for technical accuracy)

[40 marks]

Language terms	Explanation
abstract noun	a noun that relates to feelings, concepts or states that do not exist physically (e.g. hope, love)
anecdote	a short, usually entertaining story about a personal experience, used to make a point
conjunction	a word that links two words or phrases together; there are two types: coordinating conjunctions and subordinating conjunctions
connective	a word such as 'however' or 'moreover', used to link paragraphs or sentences and show the relationship between them
connotation	an idea or feeling that a word creates
convention	a particular feature or technique used in a text
direct address	when a feature of the text specifically connects with the reader
direct speech	when the words of a speaker are used in a text, using the exact words spoken
emotive language	language chosen especially to create an emotional response in the reader
headline	the heading at the top of an article
homophone	words that sound the same but are spelt differently and have different meanings
hyperbole	when the writer exaggerates their description for effect
metaphor	an image describing one thing as if it were something else that it resembles in some way
mnemonic	a memory aid, a rhyme or short sentence using the first letter of each word
parallelism	achieving contrast by repeating a grammatical formation
paraphrasing	expressing the meaning of a phrase or sentence in different words
personification	describing an object or idea as though it were human, with human feelings and attributes
register	the style of language based on choice of vocabulary and grammar
reported speech	an account of what has been said, without using the exact words spoken
rhetorical question	a question asked for effect, rather than to elicit an answer
simile	when one thing is compared directly with another using 'like' or 'as'
Standard English	the widely accepted form of English, most often used in formal and spoken speech and writing
strapline	a subheading or caption in an article
tone	the writer's apparent attitude towards the subject, e.g. humorous, angry, critical or passionate
topic sentence	a sentence that expresses the main idea of a paragraph, sometimes the first of the paragraph
tricolon	using three words or phrases in a row for effect
voice	the speaker in a text, presenting their thoughts, feelings, ideas or attitudes
viewpoint	the ideas and attitudes of the writer shown in the text

ANSWERS

Note that the sample paragraphs given here provide only one possible approach to each task. Many other approaches would also be valid and appropriate.

SECTION A: READING

Identifying correct information – Now you try! (page 7)

B The writer thinks that food is no longer cooked in the oven.

F The writer was not allowed to choose which TV channel to watch.

G The writer always argued with her brother whilst waiting for her dinner.

H The writer and her brother annoyed their father as he tried to watch TV.

Summarising and synthesising – Now you try! (page 11)

In addition to feeling frustrated, the writer in Source A also gets angry whilst waiting for dinner. She ends up in a 'full on fight' with her sibling which leads to her 'dad shouting'. This implies that waiting for her dinner is a very negative experience that leads to conflict in her family.
Source B is very different to this as the hostess has to hide her feelings and pretend that she is calm. The text says that she has to be tactful and 'must display no kind of agitation'. This implies that, underneath, the hostess might be feeling just as stressed and frustrated as the writer in Source A, but she is not allowed to show this.

Quoting and paraphrasing – Now you try! (page 13)

In the last sentence it tells us that the hostess is very worried about whether all the different aspects of her dinner, including the arrival of the guests and the roles of the cook and the servants, will come together to be successful.
The last sentence shows the 'anxiety' of the hostess during this 'trying time'; the list that the writer uses emphasises all the different elements that could go wrong, including the arrival of her guests in 'due time' and her 'trust' in both her cook and servants.

Analysing language – Now you try! (page 15)

The use of the connective 'however' indicates to the reader that the frustration of the writer continues. This is also reinforced by the metaphor 'ritual' which suggests a formal ceremony to the reader. 'Ritual' has negative connotations here as it suggests to the reader that the same processes are followed strictly every week, despite, we assume, some awareness on the parents' part of how their children are suffering. The reader empathises with the feeling of powerlessness that is conveyed through this description.

Comparing and contrasting – Putting it into practice (pages 16–19)

Source A	Source B	Source A	Source B
Perspectives/ feelings	Evidence/ methods	Perspectives/ feelings	Evidence/ methods
Changes perspective; there's a sense of excitement with microwave and fast food	• Rhetorical questions • 'You can have your chips NOW!'	The writer uses a poem to reinforce the feelings of those waiting for the food	• 'sad' • 'gloom' • 'our pain'
Change in feelings again; there's a sense of regret that people no longer eat together	• 'fast forward' over 'fondest memories' • 'it is time to slow down and smell the gravy'	The text continues to be forceful, using modal verbs like 'should'	• 'duty' to make her guests feel 'happy, comfortable and quite at their ease' • Modal verb 'should' expresses obligation

Comparing and contrasting – Now you try! (page 19)

The tone in the second paragraph of Source A shifts to emphasise the writer's increasing frustration. She seems to get angry with her family, with the alliterative phrase 'full-on fight' being used to illustrate how much her frustration has grown. The reader can empathise with the writer as they may also have been in this family situation. This makes the final statement in the second paragraph 'happy domesticity' particularly effective. The sarcastic tone here reiterates to the reader that the situation is far from happy.
In contrast, Source B continues with its controlling tone, encouraging the reader to hide their emotions and focus on their guests. The use of the modal verb 'must' reinforces this; the hostess is instructed to hide her emotions and be 'light and cheerful'. These positive adjectives convey a sense of happiness and a positive atmosphere, which the reader is clearly being told they must create in this instructional text.

Quick revision – Quick quiz (page 20)

1. Four. **2.** A specific extract as outlined in the question. **3.** A summary is when you identify the key points in a text. **4.** Synthesis is when you combine ideas or information from different sources to make a new text. **5.** Use speech marks around quoted words, only quote what is necessary, embed fluently, analyse and develop ideas. **6.** Quoting: using the exact words used, in quotation marks. Paraphrasing: putting the information into your own words. **7.** Question 2. **8.** Questions 3 and 4. **9.** Language. **10.** A specific extract as outlined in the question. **11.** Answers will vary but may include techniques, alliteration, first-person narrative, rhetorical question, exclamation, metaphor. **12.** Comparing the viewpoint, attitudes or ideas in both sources. **13.** The writer's opinion or attitude towards the topic of the writing. **14.** Language/structure/voice/point of view/register/tone. **15.** 5 minutes.

Quick revision – Practise your skills (page 21)

A Riding is a very important part of the writer's life.
C The writer likes to spend a long time riding her horse.

Quick revision – Power paragraphs (page 21)

The writer describes how dangerous he thinks the weather is. The use of the comparative adjective 'denser', in his description of the fog being 'denser than ever before', suggests that the weather is worsening. This is reinforced by the metaphor in the next line, implying that the fog is so thick you could 'almost stand on it', which gives the impression that the fog is becoming solid, conveying the writer's sense of being trapped. By adding a subordinate clause in the final line, the writer further emphasises his feeling of isolation and loneliness and how he 'felt himself drifting' because the fog has completely encompassed him. In addition, the metaphor of the 'insect on a straw' is used to exaggerate how insignificant and powerless he feels. This image combining the smallest of creatures, an 'insect', with the fragility of the straw to which it clings, shows how vulnerable he is to the elements on the open ocean.

SECTION B: BASIC WRITING SKILLS

Varying sentence types – Now you try! (page 31)

Reading – is it a skill that we need for the future? In this age of digital media, reading is no longer a popular pastime. You might disagree, but studies show that most people don't. One survey suggested that only 40% of secondary age students read in their spare time. In addition to this, research also suggested that borrowing books from libraries has fallen by 30%. It seems that the times have moved on and that reading is no longer a popular pastime.

Using sentences for different purposes – Now you try! (page 35)

There <u>should be</u> higher discounts on coach and train tickets for students. This is the policy in other countries and so <u>could be</u> done here. We <u>can</u> campaign for this and make a difference.

Using punctuation and forms of speech – Now you try! (page 39)

Having a pet is so overrated; I really do not know what all the fuss is about. Pets can take over your life: they are messy so you have to constantly clean up, they

can cost a fortune (in food, toys and vet's bills), and they sometimes even destroy your home. Why would you want to tie yourself down and limit your holiday opportunities for the sake of a pet?

Using paragraphs and connectives – Now you try! (page 41)

In addition, many business leaders have expressed growing concern over the skills of school leavers. The increased focus on preparing for exams is not producing people that can be successful in the workplace; how many times do you think employees are asked to complete a multiple-choice test in timed conditions at work? In a recent interview about secondary education, the CEO of the global company Cybercore commented, 'This ridiculous focus on exams is creating a huge problem for employers; we want creative thinkers, not robots'. Business leaders and students agree; it is time for a change.

Spelling – Now you try! (page 43)

Rats can make great pets as they're very sociable and friendly. As long as you are mindful that rats love climbing and jumping, they are manageable. They seem to be misunderstood by many families and it's an unfair situation.

Quick revision – Quick quiz (page 44)

1. A simple sentence contains only a subject and a verb, and sometimes also an object. **2.** A compound sentence joins two simple sentences using a coordinating conjunction, e.g. 'and', 'but', 'or', 'nor', 'so' or 'yet'. **3.** A complex sentence includes a main clause, which makes sense on its own, and at least one subordinate clause, which only makes sense in relation to the main clause. **4.** A declarative sentence makes a statement about someone or something.
5. An interrogative sentence requests information, so you might use it to make the reader think about their understanding of the topic you are trying to explain.
6. An exclamatory sentence has an exclamation mark and indicates strong feelings. **7.** An imperative sentence is a command in which the subject (second person 'you', singular or plural) is left out.
8. You would mainly use the present tense when writing to give a viewpoint. **9.** A comma separates the main clause in a sentence from the subordinate clause. A comma can also be used to separate items in a list or a series of descriptions. **10.** A semicolon links two ideas, events or pieces of information. Semicolons can also be used to separate items in a long list.
11. Round brackets are used to include extra information or an afterthought without altering the meaning of the sentence. **12.** You might use reported speech to describe the opinions of experts or when telling an anecdote. **13.** A new paragraph should be used to indicate a change of idea, topic, place or time. **14.** A range of answers are possible (see the table on page 40). **15.** their = belonging to them; there = that place; they're = shortened form of 'they are'.

ANSWERS

Quick revision - Practise your skills (page 45)

Swimming is an essential skill that all children need in their lives. Why is swimming important, you ask? Imagine the number of times that you have used this skill; swimming could quite literally save your life! It is also great exercise – a fun way to keep fit and active.

Quick revision - Power paragraphs (page 45)

Have you ever wondered why being allowed to wear jewellery is such an important issue in schools? Jewellery has long been a way to express yourself. For instance, a necklace or earrings can show that you are individual; make you feel special. Why do schools insist on controlling students so that they can't even choose what earrings they wear?

In addition, jewellery can also have personal significance. A gift from a loved one can bring comfort. Why should students be prevented from that comfort just because they are in school?

SECTION B: VIEWPOINT WRITING

Non-fiction text types - Now you try! (page 49)

Thank you all for coming today to listen to my ideas regarding the important topic of phone use in schools. Technology is a powerful force shaping all aspects of our modern lives, not just in schools. Phones are a tool to help us learn, but we must be careful that we do not let them dominate every waking moment. What is their main function? Is it learning? I think we would all agree that it isn't, and that phones are a distraction to us all in school.

Purpose, audience and form - Now you try! (page 51)

Form – article; audience – magazine; purpose – argue for or against this statement; register – formal (to be published in a magazine) but may also be conversational due to the topic; tone – passionate (either for or against) and might include humour. Possible opening paragraph:

REALITY TV REACHES NEW LOWS

Reality TV – a waste of time for all of us

Just when you thought the media had run out of new ideas, up pops a new reality TV show that grips the nation, propelling its participants to stardom in an instant. Is it time to 'call time' on this unoriginal format? Yes it is!

Persuasive language techniques - Now you try! (page 53)

Any student will tell you how uncomfortable school uniform can be. Hot, itchy and ill fitting, it can make a full day at school torturous, especially in extreme temperatures. Why would any parent want to expose their child to this sort of suffering? I remember last summer, the temperature was so high that the school had to let students change into their PE kit.

Persuading effectively - Now you try! (page 55)

A tax on sugar is the best way forward if we want to solve this problem. The problem may seem like a huge mountain to climb, but the sugar tax is the first step on this long journey. If all groups work together – parents, children and manufacturing companies – we can defeat this evil and improve the health of our country. The tax is just the first step; educating children and changing the way that school dinners are provided are our next hurdles in this battle to make Britain healthier and happier.

Structuring an argument - Now you try! (page 57)

Is veganism a healthy way of life? Yes. Should schools promote and encourage it? No, in my view. Students should have the right to make their own lifestyle choices, without feeling under pressure to subscribe to a particular point of view because it is the latest fad. A vegan diet may be a healthy lifestyle choice, but it could also present risks if not followed properly. Students of our age are growing rapidly, and could miss out on essential vitamins and minerals, like calcium for example, if they stop eating dairy foods and meat. It may mean they help to save the environment; but at what cost to themselves?

Quick revision - Quick quiz (pages 58-59)

1. Letter. **2.** Article and leaflet. **3.** Leaflet. **4.** When you use 'you' or 'your' to address the reader to engage them and persuade them to listen to your argument or to take action. **5.** Purpose: what the writing is intended to do; audience: who it is aimed at; form: where the writing will appear. **6.** Register is the type of language that indicates how formal the text type is. **7.** Tone is the writer's apparent attitude towards the subject, e.g. humorous, angry, critical or passionate. **8.** Answers could include rhetorical questions, tricolon, alliteration, personification, parallelism. **9.** Tricolon is when you use three words in a row that have a similar meaning for effect. **10.** Statistics, anecdotes and quotations from 'experts'. **11.** They both compare. A simile uses the word 'like' or 'as' to compare; a metaphor says that something is something else. **12.** At the beginning of each paragraph. **13.** Answers could include: however, similarly, firstly, in addition, finally, in contrast. **14.** One. **15.** When you move on to the next point

Quick revision - Practise your skills (page 59)

- Connectives could be added where indicated with the asterisks below.
- A rhetorical device or persuasive language could replace the underlined section.
- More evidence could be shown for how many handouts are given out and/or lost, and/or how much paper could be saved.

I do think that schools waste too much paper. *Teachers are constantly giving out handouts that students then lose. Why can't these be shared online? *Students could work on phones or tablets, which would mean that we would no longer need to use paper in school.

ANSWERS

Quick revision - Power paragraphs (page 59)

1. Possible paragraph:

The way schools waste paper is like throwing both our money and our environment down the drain. For instance, teachers are constantly giving out handouts that students then lose. 80% of students said that they never use handouts again or that they lose them. Why can't these be shared online? Alternatively, students could work on their computers in school, which would mean that we would no longer need to use paper.

2. Possible paragraph:

Did you know that every day supermarkets throw away food that is worth more than £50,000? EVERY DAY! Some charities have started to take this food and reuse it, but this is only the tip of the iceberg. Most of the food is perfectly fine to eat – it has just passed its sell-by date. People are living on the streets and going hungry while food sits abandoned in bins behind supermarkets. This has to stop.

SECTION B: EXAM PRACTICE

Grade 5 sample answer - Check your skills (page 67)

Sport is exciting, enjoyable and fun. Why wouldn't you want to join in? Most importantly, it helps us all stay healthy, ensuring that we are in good health for later life. Schools must keep compulsory sports so that all students can benefit from joining in.

Grade 7+ sample answer - Check your skills (page 69)

A05
- Ideas are generally clear in the first response and consistently clear in the second response.
- There is a wider range of language devices in the second response, including persuasive rhetorical question.
- The style and register are consistent.
- The ideas are clearly connected together.

A06
- There is a variety of sentence forms and punctuation, with a more sophisticated use of vocabulary.

Grade 7+ sample answer - Now you try! (page 69)

For many, sport should be an opportunity for self-expression. But where is the freedom to express yourself when you are forced to play rugby on a wet and windy winter's afternoon? Sport should be removed from the curriculum in schools; it has become a symbol of draconian punishment for most, inspiring fear and dread in even the fittest and most sporting of students.

Everyone can think of a time when they have enjoyed physical activity with others – playing tennis with friends on a sunny afternoon, walking the dog or coming home covered in mud after playing football

in the park with friends. This feeling of enjoyment and fun, however, is not a feeling that I associate with compulsory sports at school. The freedom to have fun is what we need to inspire our students to feel when they are involved in sports, something that compulsory sports just cannot provide.

Sport in school seems to focus solely on team games. It is true that these games can promote a sense of community and interaction with others; but this can also be a source of conflict between students. Statistics show that bullying between students is 40% more likely in sports lessons than in classroom lessons. Why do we let this happen? It is time to rethink our approach to sport in schools so that all students feel safe.

Consequently, compulsory sports lessons have become a time of dread for many students. Stephen from Hull said, 'I used to hate sports lessons at school. From getting changed to the picking of teams, the whole thing was humiliating for me as I was just not very good at sports.' Stephen's story is true for many students; feeling fear and dread is not going to encourage them to enjoy sport, either at school or in later life.

How can we change things for the better? There is no easy solution to this problem, especially when you consider the limitations placed on the school curriculum by issues like school funding. However, it is time for a radical overhaul. Professor Smith of the University of Leicester has been trialling a voluntary sports programme that focuses on students choosing their own sports and the level of participation. So far, his research has shown increases in student motivation and attitudes to sport. This shows us that if we listen to young people we can find the solution to this issue. Ultimately, sport should be accessible, fun and good for our short- and long-term health. So many of us think of negative experiences when we consider compulsory sports in schools; it is time for this to change. Listen to young people, consult them and give them responsibility and choices; only then will you be able to develop a sports curriculum that will ensure that students continue to see exercise and fitness as important in their later lives.

Thank you for listening.

Practice Paper 2 - Section A: Reading (pages 73-4)

1. True: B, C, E, G.

2. Both sources describe how they make arrangements to make people comfortable and happy at Christmas. Source B explains how Christmas dinner is provided for the poor people of London with food that is much better than the poor people would expect: 'No skilly to-day – but beef!' This suggests that the organisers really care about making the day special. Source A also describes how the Abbeyfield care homes arrange for lonely elderly people to be involved in 'activities, meals and overnight stays'. The article explains how the overnight stay means that the elderly people won't wake up alone on Christmas Day, which suggests that the organisers understand how difficult it can be to be alone at Christmas.

3. In Source B, the writer uses repetition of 'genial' and 'geniality' to convey the positive atmosphere of the day. The connotations of 'genial' are kindness and cheerfulnesss, which is also echoed in the description 'cheerful' bustle. The writer also uses personification of Christmas, who 'finds them out', which suggests that Christmas is determined to involve everyone in the celebrations.

4. The perspective of Source A is clear that Christmas is a time to involve everyone and caring for lonely people is part of this. The writer uses the tricolon 'our residents, their families and older people from the community'; this list emphasises how important it is to include everyone in the celebrations. This is also reinforced by the use of the word 'community', which suggests inclusion and participation for all. Source B also presents how important it is to include everyone in the celebrations. The use of statistics at the beginning of the article reinforces this viewpoint, with 'some eighty to a hundred thousand' having meals provided for them.

The writer uses personification of Christmas to emphasise the passion of the organisers: Christmas 'finds ... out' the poor and sick people, which suggests the view that they are determined to involve as many people as possible in the Christmas celebrations.

Practice Paper 2 – Section B: Writing (page 74)

5. **Grade 5 opening to sample response**
It's celebration time!
Religious festivities should be happy times of the year that focus on families. It is time to change our attitudes and stop spending large amounts of money on presents that people don't need. It's time for a change – don't you agree? With households spending huge amounts on unnecessary gifts, such festivities are getting out of hand. Many gifts cost money that families cannot afford. The constant advertising of festive gifts, new toys or games reaches ridiculous levels at such times, with children nagging their parents constantly.

5. **Grade 7+ opening to sample response**
Charity begins at home?
The festive season is a time for giving. That is certainly what all the adverts say. But, giving what exactly? It's time that we review our attitudes to the festivals we celebrate and offer, instead, the gift of time, companionship and affection rather than disposable plastic or wads of cash. Shopping has reached frenzied heights: households spend record sums year on year; pressure is put on families by constant advertising; everyone tries to match what neighbours or relatives lavish on each other. Religious festivities can now seem to stand in a moral vacuum. So, what happened to more traditional ideals? Hope. Kindness. Love. And most of all, charity. Let's choose to do more small acts of charity and kindness.